Routledge Revivals

The Pure Theory of International Trade and Distortions

First published in 1978. This book provides a simple, systematic, yet rigorous treatment of the key aspects of the pure theory of international trade and distortions. The opening chapter presents the standard two-factor, two-commodity barter model of international trade and a comprehensive treatment of the important properties and relationships. The rest of the book consists of four sections: parts One and Two are devoted to an analysis of factor market imperfections, and parts Three and Four consider the trade-theoretical consequences of product market imperfections. A concluding chapter presents some generalised theorems. This book will be of interest to students of economics.

The Pure Theory of International Trade and Distortions

Bharat R. Hazari

Routledge
Taylor & Francis Group

First published in 1978
by Croom Helm

This edition first published in 2016 by Routledge
2 Park Square, Milton Park, Abingdon, Oxon, OX14 4RN
and by Routledge
711 Third Avenue, New York, NY 10017

Routledge is an imprint of the Taylor & Francis Group, an informa business

© 1978 Bharat R. Hazari

Publisher's Note
The publisher has gone to great lengths to ensure the quality of this reprint but points out that some imperfections in the original copies may be apparent.

Disclaimer
The publisher has made every effort to trace copyright holders and welcomes correspondence from those they have been unable to contact.

A Library of Congress record exists under LC control number: 89033996

ISBN 13: 978-1-138-64463-2 (hbk)
ISBN 13: 978-1-315-62866-0 (ebk)
ISBN 13: 978-1-138-64468-7 (pbk)

The Pure Theory of International Trade and Distortions

BHARAT R. HAZARI

CROOM HELM LONDON

©1978 Bharat R. Hazari
Croom Helm Ltd, 2–10 St John's Road, London SW11

British Library Cataloguing in Publication Data

Hazari, Bharat R.
    The pure theory of international trade and
    distortions.
    1. Commerce
    I. Title
    382'.01   HF81

    ISBN 0-85664-441-2

Printed in Great Britain by offset lithography by
Billing & Sons Ltd, Guildford, London and Worcester

ACKNOWLEDGEMENTS

My greatest intellectual debt is to my two distinguished teachers and
thesis supervisors at Harvard University, Professors Richard E. Caves and
Hendrik S. Houthakker. Both of them were kind enough to comment
on an earlier draft of this book.

I recall with great pleasure the intellectual stimulus provided by my
distinguished teacher, Professor Jagdish Bhagwati, at the Delhi School
of Economics. He is partly responsible for my interest in the pathological
cases associated with trade and distortion theory.

Thanks are also due to my colleagues, Mr P. M. Sgro and Mr W.
Horrigan, and my student, Mr D. C. Suh, for their comments, insights
and questions. Comments received from Professor Ajit K. Dasgupta of
the Institute of Economic Growth, Delhi, on an earlier draft of the
book are much appreciated.

Also deserving of very special thanks are Mrs Jane Morris and Mrs
Janet Peggie who suffered the difficulties of typing this manuscript,
womanfully!

Finally, I am grateful to my wife, Savita, who cheerfully bore much
more than her fair share of responsibility for looking after our daughter
Amaruka in Paris to make maximum time available for my research.

This book has been written during my sabbatical leave which I
spent at the Indian Statistical Institute, Delhi, the Laboratoire
d'Econometrie de L'Ecole Polytechnique, Paris, and at Harvard
University. Of these institutes L'Ecole Polytechnique provided me with
an excellent environment for writing this book.

The responsibility for errors and omissions rests with me.

Bharat R. Hazari

TO MY FATHER

CONTENTS

INTRODUCTION

(1) Subject-Matter of the Pure Theory of International Trade

The theory of international trade is traditionally divided into two branches: pure and monetary.[1] The former analyses issues of international economics which abstract from Keynesian problems of determining the price level and employment. This pure or real theory of international trade is generally cast in terms of simple general equilibrium models, especially the so-called two-by-two-by-two version of the Heckscher—Ohlin model (two commodities, two factors, two countries). Within this broad framework the real theory of trade deals with two different classes of questions, namely, positive and normative.

On the positive side the pure theory discusses, *inter alia*, the determination of the pattern of trade; the effect of economic expansion on output levels and terms of trade; the impact of an *ad valorem* tariff on (a) the internal and external prices and (b) on the internal distribution of income; and the equalisation of factor prices in the absence of international mobility of factors.

In similar fashion numerous issues have been analysed in the welfare branch of the real theory of international trade. Among them are the welfare ranking of free trade versus autarky; the optimality or otherwise of the policy of *laissez-faire*; the impact of economic expansion on welfare; the welfare ranking of a higher versus a lower tariff; and the optimal commercial policy in the presence of non-economic objectives.

(2) Purpose of the Book

In the past decade the entire subject of the pure theory of trade was surveyed by several distinguished economists.[2] A number of exceedingly good textbooks also appeared on this topic.[3] However, an area about which very few full-length treatments have been published is the pure theory of trade and distortions.[4] It was after the publication of the justly celebrated paper of Haberler (10) in 1950 that distortions received increasing attention from trade theorists.[5] While in the fifties only a few papers appeared, the decades of the sixties and seventies witnessed mushrooming growth in the literature on distortion and trade theory. The present work aims at providing a simple, systematic, but rigorous treatment of the relatively more important aspects of the pure theory of trade and distortions in book form.

1

(3) Tools of Analysis Used in the Book

The exposition of theory in the text relies on both mathematics (simple calculus) and diagrams. Algebraic analysis has been used mainly for two reasons. First, algebra helps one in understanding many non-intuitive and interesting results in trade and distortion theory (which abounds in such results). Second, algebraic analysis points to its own generalisations. The very liberal use of geometry in the present work is motivated by three main considerations: first, the heavy use of geometry historically in the pure theory of trade; second, to make the book accessible to senior undergraduates, some of whom may not have been trained in mathematical analysis; third, geometry and English (or any other language) provide adequate tools for presenting almost all the results in trade and distortion theory which are based on the two-factor, two-commodity model of international trade. Calculus and geometry have been used together, except in Chapter 6 and parts of Chapters 7 and 10 which have been developed in geometrical terms only. Wherever mathematics and geometry are used simultaneously, algebraic results always precede the geometrical presentation. A trade theorist who does not relish mathematics can avoid the algebra and read the entire book in terms of geometry and English. However, the mathematically oriented reader will have to learn some geometry to comprehend the book in its entirety.

(4) Organisation of the Book and Some Comments on Distortions

In Chapter 1, the standard two-factor, two-commodity barter model of international trade is presented. As most results in trade and distortion theory are derived from this model,[6] a comprehensive treatment of the important properties and key relationships is also provided. It is also shown in this chapter that under first best assumptions[7] the Pareto optimum position is characterised by the equality between the domestic rate of substitution in consumption (DRS), the domestic rate of transformation in production (DRT) and the foreign rate of transformation (FRT), i.e. DRS = DRT = FRT. This is an important equality because a large number of distortions have a bearing on the equality between these rates.

The rest of the book is divided into four parts in which the consequences of various types of distortions are discussed. In the present work distortions are invariably defined in terms of the source. This contrasts with the approach adopted by Bhagwati (4) in his classic paper on distortion theory, where distortions are defined in terms of consequences. Bhagwati defines four principal types of distortions, namely (i) FRT ≠ DRT = DRS; (ii) DRT ≠ DRS = FRT; (iii) DRS ≠ DRT = FRT and (iv) non-operation on the efficient production possibility curve. Thus, the number of distortions is determined not in terms of intuitive sources of distortions but in terms of consequences. This approach is not satisfactory from an analytical point of view though unobjectionable as an operational concept. It is better to define distortions in terms of what they are rather than in terms of what they do. One is interested in looking for a definition that starts earlier in the process, one that identifies the economic phenomenon leading to the postulated violation of the optimality condition. Hence, in the present work distortions are defined from the source.

Parts One and Two of the book are devoted to an analysis of factor market imperfections. Traditionally trade theorists have been interested in the consequences of two different but not mutually exclusive types of factor market imperfections, namely factor price differentials and minimum real wage rates. Distortionary factor price differentials involve the non-uniform payment to an identical factor in different sectors of the economy. In other words, the factor price differential cannot be attributed to legitimate economic grounds such as disutility in occupations.

In Part One, we examine the trade-theoretic consequences of the presence of the distortionary factor price differentials. This part consists of four chapters (2–5) in which both positive and normative consequences of the presence of factor price differentials are discussed.[8] For instance, among the positive consequences analysed are: the importance of the distinction between physical factor intensities and value factor intensities, the relation between commodity price changes and output changes, and the impact of technical progress on output level and terms of trade. Similarly, several welfare propositions have been analysed in the presence of factor price differentials, for example the three theorems on gains from trade and the phenomenon of 'immiserising growth'.

Part Two looks at the consequences upon trade theory of the other type of factor market distortion, that is the presence of a minimum real wage rate in the economy. Two alternative specifications of the minimum real wage rate are considered: (i) a uniform minimum real wage that prevails in both sectors of the economy; and (ii) a minimum real wage rate in the urban sector of the economy. The wage in the second sector (rural) is equated with the expected wage rate. The imposition of a minimum real wage rate implies that the wage cannot be bid down (once it becomes a binding constraint) to the competitive level to ensure full employment. Hence, in the presence of this type of distortion full employment is not necessarily ensured. The presence of type (i) minimum real wage generally results in unemployment that is not specific to any sector, type (ii) wage specification results in sector-specific unemployment. Our focus of attention in the two chapters in this part of the book is on unemployment and welfare. Chapter 6 is devoted to examining the consequences of type (i) and chapter 7 type (ii) minimum real wage rate.

In Parts Three and Four the trade-theoretic consequences of product market imperfections are considered. Throughout the first two parts of the book the product markets are assumed to be perfectly competitive. In Parts Three and Four it is factor markets which are assumed to be perfectly competitive. Since we are working on the basis of an open model, there are two product markets, domestic and foreign. The consequences of distortions in the domestic market are analysed in Part Three, while Part Four develops the consequences of a distorted foreign market.

Two types of product market imperfections are considered in Part Three, namely pure production externality of the Meade variety and domestic monopoly. In Chapter 8, we consider among other things the welfare ranking of free trade versus no trade, the Rybczynski theorem and the welfare effects of economic expansion, in the presence of a Meade-type production externality. Chapter 9 is devoted to an analysis of monopoly in a model of international trade. Three issues are considered in this chapter – the existence of an autarky equilibrium, the welfare ranking of free trade *vis-à-vis* no trade and the Lerner symmetry theorem in the presence of a domestic monopoly.

Part Four concentrates on the relatively more important consequences of the impositions of a tariff in the small country case. The imposition of a tariff in a country facing fixed terms of trade creates a distortion because in such a country tariff is not the optimal policy. Despite their suboptimality tariffs are widely used for reasons that cannot be justified on legitimate economic grounds in the context of a small country. Tariffs in less developed countries often result in smuggling. Part of Chapter 10 analyses the welfare effects of smuggling in the presence of a tariff. The rest of the chapter is devoted to an analysis of welfare consequences of economic expansion in the presence of tariffs without smuggling.

Finally, in Chapter 11, some generalised theorems on international trade and distortion theory are presented.

Notes

1. This distinction was originally drawn by Marshall (17).
2. These surveys have been conducted by Bhagwati (1964) (2), Caves (1960) (5), Chipman (1965) (7), Corden (1965) (8), Haberler (1961) (11) and Mundell (1960) (19).
3. See, for instance, Caves and Jones (6) and Kemp (14).
4. There are three relatively long and general treatments of trade and distortion theory, namely, Bhagwati (4), Corden (9) and Magee (15), (16). Bhagwati's masterly treatment is devoted to considering only the welfare part of trade and distortion theory. Corden's otherwise excellent work is in a partial equilibrium framework which is not in vogue with the current generation of trade theorists. Magee's extremely competent survey is only concerned with factor market imperfections and does not consider the consequences of other types of distortions. In this context the book of Batra (1) should also be mentioned because it contains some chapters on distortion and trade theory. The present book considers the implications of various distortions and is cast in terms of a general equilibrium model which is currently in use by trade theorists. General treatments which contain some discussion of distortion theory, for instance, are Bhagwati (2), Caves (5) and Kemp (14).
5. The normative part of trade and distortion theory is often classified as belonging to the theory of second best.
6. Some results on trade and distortion theory have also been obtained in a three-commodity model in which one good is non-traded. See for instance Batra (1), Hazari and Sgro (12), (13).
7. An excellent treatment of the distinction between first best and second best assumptions is available in Bhagwati (3), footnote, page 71.
8. A number of results in Chapters 3–5 are taken from the author's doctoral dissertation at Harvard University, which was submitted in 1972.

References

(1) Batra, R. N. 1973. *Studies in the Pure Theory of International Trade*. London: Macmillan.
(2) Bhagwati, J. N. 1964. The Pure Theory of International Trade: A Survey. *Economic Journal*, 74 (March), 1–84.
(3) Bhagwati, J. N. 1969. *Trade, Tariffs and Growth*. London: Weidenfeld and Nicolson.
(4) Bhagwati, J. N. 1971. The Generalized Theory of Distortions and Welfare. In J. N. Bhagwati *et al.* (eds.), *Trade, Balance of Payments and Growth*. Papers in International Economics in Honour of C. P. Kindleberger. Amsterdam: North Holland.
(5) Caves, R. E. 1960. *Trade and Economic Structure*. Cambridge, Massachusetts: Harvard University Press.
(6) Caves, R. E., and Jones, R. W. 1973. *World Trade and Payments: An Introduction*. Boston: Little, Brown.
(7) Chipman, J. S. 1965, 1965 and 1966. A Survey of the Theory of International Trade. *Econometrica*, Vol. 33 (July), 477–519; Vol. 33 (October), 685–760; and Vol. 34 (January), 18–76.
(8) Corden, W. M. 1965. *Recent Developments in the Theory of International Trade*. Special Papers in International Economics No. 7. Princeton: International Finance Section.

(9) Corden, W. M. 1974. *Trade Policy and Economic Welfare*. Oxford: Clarendon Press.

(10) Haberler, G. 1950. Some Problems in the Pure Theory of International Trade. *Economic Journal*, Vol. 60 (June), 223–40.

(11) Haberler, G. 1961. *A Survey of International Trade Theory*. Special Papers in International Economics, No. 1. Revised edition. Princeton: International Finance Section.

(12) Hazari, B. R., and Sgro, P. M. 1975. Theorems on Immiserizing (Normal Growth) in the Non-Traded Goods and Wage Differentials Framework. *Southern Economic Journal*, Vol. 41 (January), 515–19.

(13) Hazari, B. R., and Sgro, P. M. 1976. Some Notes on Technical Progress in the Framework of Factor Market Imperfections and Non-Traded Goods. *Australian Economic Papers*, Vol. 16 (June), 76–86.

(14) Kemp, M. C. 1969. *The Pure Theory of International Trade and Investment*. Englewood Cliffs, New Jersey: Prentice-Hall.

(15) Magee, S. P. 1973. Factor Market Distortions, Production and Trade: A Survey. *Oxford Economic Papers*, Vol. 25 (March), 1–43.

(16) Magee, S. P. 1976. *International Trade and Distortions in Factor Markets*. Business Economics and Finance Series, Vol. 6. New York and Base: Marcel Dekker.

(17) Marshall, A. 1949. *The Pure Theory of Foreign Trade*. London: London School of Economics and Political Science.

(18) Meade, J. E. 1952. External Economies and Diseconomies in a Competitive Situation. *Economic Journal*, Vol. 62 (March), 54–67.

(19) Mundell, R. A. (1960). The Pure Theory of International Trade. *American Economic Review*, Vol. 50 (March), 67–110.

1 A MODEL OF A TRADING WORLD

This chapter presents the standard two-commodity, two-factor barter model of international trade that will be used throughout the present book.[1] In this part we shall be mainly engaged in the construction of a formal model of a trading economy and discussing its relatively more important properties. Since the pure theory of international trade makes heavy use of several concepts of micro-economics, a brief treatment of the more frequently used micro-economics concepts is also provided. The closed economy model can easily be derived as a subset of the open economy model presented in this chapter.[2]

1.1 The Formal Model

We consider a country which produces two commodities, X_1 and X_2. The utility function for the country as a whole is given by:

$$U = U(D_1, D_2) \tag{1.1}$$

where U indicates utility and D_1 and D_2 the domestic consumption of commodities X_1 and X_2. The utility function is assumed to be strictly concave. The social indifference curves associated with the utility function equation (1.1) are presented in Figure 1.1. These curves are assumed to be convex to the origin and non-intersecting.

At this point it is important to remind the reader that the assumption of the existence of a well behaved aggregate utility function is indeed a strong one. This is so because of the problems associated in going from individual indifference maps to social indifference maps. Undoubtedly, under a set of very restrictive assumptions this can be done. For example, if all individuals have identical tastes and endowments, then the aggregation of individual indifference curves generates social indifference curves which possess the same properties as the individual indifference curves. The assumption of identical tastes need not be regarded as outrageous, since the aggregation is performed over the set of individuals that belong to a particular nation, and hence involves cultural similarities. However, there is no denying the fact that the assumption of identical endowment for each consumer is indeed a very strong one.

Given the rather stringent assumptions under which an aggregate utility function can be generated, one may legitimately ask the question,

Figure 1.1

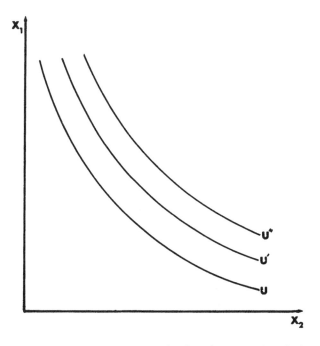

why use a utility function at all? If one's interest is only in positive economics (more specifically positive propositions in trade theory), then one need not use a utility function that possesses both behavioural and welfare significance. However, if one is interested in making welfare judgements about society as a whole, one immediately needs a well behaved utility function. If the economist is interested in comparing the welfare effects of a lower tariff with a higher tariff, then a utility function is needed. Economists do like making policy judgements and policy recommendations, and hence, in spite of difficulties associated with the aggregate utility function, this concept is used very widely. In the present book an aggregate utility function will be used to establish normative results.

Given utility maximisation, the following condition can be easily derived:

$$\frac{U_2}{U_1} = \frac{p_2}{p_1} \tag{1.2}$$

where $U_i = \partial U/\partial D_i$ ($i = 1, 2$). This condition states that in equilibrium the marginal rate of substitution in consumption equals the ratio of commodity prices. This condition is the national counterpart of the condition of individual maximisation in the theory of consumer behaviour.

It is assumed that part of X_1 is exported and part of X_2 is imported, so that:

$$D_1 = X_1 - E_1 \tag{1.3}$$

$$D_2 = X_2 + M_2 \tag{1.4}$$

where X_i ($i = 1, 2$) indicates the level of output, E_1 represents the exports of commodity X_1 and M_2 represent the imports of commodity X_2. In a closed economy model the import–export terms equal zero. In economic terms this implies that all markets must clear locally. However, in an open model local excess supply or demand can be met in the international markets.

The balance of payments equilibrium requires that the following condition always be satisfied:

$$E_1 = pM_2 \tag{1.5}$$

where $p = p_2/p_1$, i.e. the relative price of commodity 2 in terms of commodity 1. This condition states that in equilibrium the value of exports must equal the value of imports.[3]

We now specify the production functions. The ith production relationship is written as:

$$X_i = F_i(K_i, L_i) \quad i = 1, 2 \tag{1.6}$$

where K_i denotes the amount of capital employed in the ith industry and L_i the amount of labour employed in the ith industry.[4] Note that we have assumed absence of externalities in specifying (1.6).

Both the factors of production are assumed to be indispensable in the production process in the following sense:

$$F_i(0, L_i) = F_i(K_i, 0) = 0 \quad i = 1, 2$$

The economic meaning of the above restriction is that both factors must be used in positive quantity to obtain a positive output.

We also assume that F_i is homogeneous of degree one in K_i and L_i, which implies that if both factors are changed in the same proportion, output also changes by the same proportion. The assumption can be stated mathematically in the following way:

$$\lambda X_i = F(\lambda K_i, \lambda L_i), \quad \lambda > 0$$

Given the assumption of homogeneity, it follows that the average product of labour depends only on the capital–labour ratio, $k_i = K_i/L_i$. Moreover, the production function can be written in its intensive form, i.e. output can be expressed as the product of a scale factor (L_i) and a function f_i of the capital–labour ratio k_i:

$$X_i = L_i F_i\left(\frac{K_i}{L_i}, 1\right) = L_i f_i(k_i) \quad i = 1, 2 \tag{1.7}$$

The marginal products of capital and labour in terms of the ith commodity respectively are given below:

$$\frac{\partial}{\partial K_i} F_i(K_i, L_i) = f_i'(k_i) \qquad i = 1, 2$$

$$\frac{\partial}{\partial L_i} F_i(K_i, L_i) = f_i(k_i) - k_i f_i'(k_i) \qquad i = 1, 2$$

Note that all marginal products depend on the capital–labour ratio. All marginal products are assumed to be positive but diminishing, hence:

$$f_i'(k_i) > 0 \quad \text{if } k_i > 0$$

$$f_i''(k_i) < 0$$

It will be assumed further that:

$$\lim_{k_i \to 0} f_i(k_i) = 0$$

$$\lim_{k_i \to \infty} f_i(k_i) = \infty$$

$$\lim_{k_i \to 0} f_i'(k_i) = \infty$$

$$\lim_{k_i \to \infty} f_i'(k_i) = 0$$

Both the factor and commodity market are assumed to be perfectly competitive. Then, given the further assumptions of profit maximisation and that both commodities are produced, it follows that the reward of each factor in equilibrium equals the value of its marginal product. Hence:

$$r = f_1' = p f_2' \tag{1.8}$$

$$w = f_1 - k_1 f_1' = p(f_2 - k_2 f_2') \tag{1.9}$$

where r denotes the rental on capital and w the wage rate. From (1.8) and (1.9) it follows that the ratio of factor rewards equals:

$$\omega \equiv \frac{w}{r} = \frac{f_i}{f_i'} - k_i \quad i = 1, 2 \tag{1.10}$$

The function $f_i(k_i)$ can be represented in terms of a simple diagram. This is done in Figure 1.2.[5] On the vertical axis we represent X_i/L_i and on the horizontal axis $k_i = K_i/L_i$. For any capital intensity k_i the equilibrium wage-rental ratio can also be read from the diagram. Suppose in Figure 1.2 the capital intensity $k_i^* = OA$. Then:

$$\omega = \frac{f_i}{f_i'} - k_i = \frac{RA}{\dfrac{RA}{AS}} - OA = OS$$

Given the homogeneity assumption there is another way of expressing the production functions. Since the marginal products of both factors depend on the factor proportions (equation 1.10), the inform-

Figure 1.2

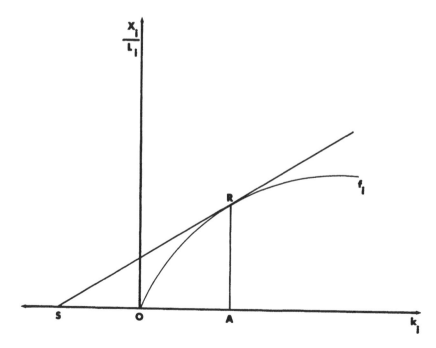

ation regarding production functions can be summed up in the two-dimensional capital and labour space by introducing unit isoquants. Suppose $\lambda = 1/X_i$. Then by homogeneity, the production functions can be written as:

$$1 = F_i(a_{Ki}, a_{Li})$$

where a_{Ki} and a_{Li} are variable Leontief input coefficients.

In Figure 1.3 unit isoquants for commodity 1 and 2 are presented. The isoquants in Figure 1.3 show the locus of various combinations of capital (K) and labour (L) that are necessary to produce one unit of X_1 and X_2. Different points on the isoquant show different capital–labour ratios, hence different marginal products of capital and labour. From equation (1.10) it follows that in equilibrium the ratio of factor rewards equals the ratio of marginal products. For an arbitrary factor

Figure 1.3

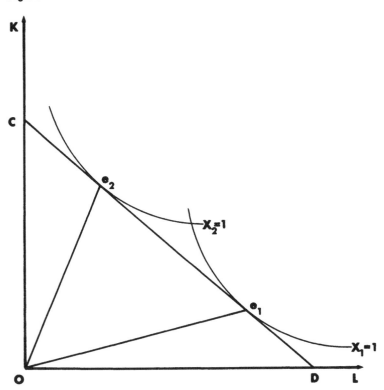

price ratio given by the slope of CD in Figure 1.3, equilibrium is attained at point e_1 for X_1 and at e_2 for X_2. At points e_1 and e_2 the capital–labour ratio equals the slopes of the lines Oe_1 and Oe_2. The marginal product of capital and labour associated with the equilibrium point e_1 are $1/OC$ and $1/OD$. Similarly for commodity 2. The price of the commodity at point e_1 equals $p_1 = w.OD = r.OC$. It is assumed in the diagram that sector 2 is capital-intensive and sector 1 labour-intensive. We also assume that at all factor prices factor intensities do not reverse.

Finally, we assume that the two primary factors of production capital (K) and labour (L) are fully employed.

$$L_1 + L_2 \quad = \bar{L} \tag{1.11}$$

$$k_1 L_1 + k_2 L_2 = \bar{K} \tag{1.12}$$

Unless otherwise specified, in equations (1.1) to (1.12) we have presented the model and its assumptions that will be used throughout the book. The model consists of a system of 16 unknowns, $U, D_1, D_2, X_1, K_1, L_1, k_1, X_2, K_2, L_2, k_2, E_1, M_2, p, r$, and w in 15 independent equations. The model is closed by assuming the country to be small, i.e. by assuming that p the terms of trade are given exogenously.[6]

The closed economy version of the model can be derived by assuming E_1 and M_2 to equal zero and by dropping the balance of payments equation. We are now in a position to derive several interesting relationships and present some important theorems that are used in later chapters.

1.2 Factor Intensities, Factor Prices and Commodity Prices

Given the restrictions on the production functions, it is obvious from equation (1.10) that k_i's are uniquely determined by the wage-rental ratio. By differentiating equation (1.10) with respect to ω the relationship between the wage–rental ratio and the sectoral capital–labour ratios can be obtained. This is given below:

$$\frac{dk_i}{d\omega} = -\frac{(f_i')^2}{f_i f_i''} > 0 \tag{1.13}$$

The economic meaning of equation (1.13) is that when wage–rental ratio rises, capital–labour ratio rises. This happens because an increase in the wage–rental ratio represents an increase in the price of labour relative to the price of capital, so that the entrepreneurs substitute capital for labour, the relatively cheaper factor for the relatively dearer

Figure 1.4

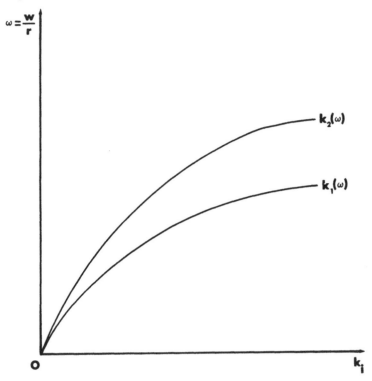

factor, leading to an increase in the capital–labour ratio. This relationship is presented in Figure 1.4, given the assumption that sector 1 is capital-intensive, $(k_1 > k_2)$. This result can also easily be derived from the isoquant diagram.

From equation (1.8), we obtain:

$$p = \frac{f_1'(k_1)}{f_2'(k_2)} \tag{1.14}$$

The right-hand side of equation (1.14) is a function of ω alone. Denoting this function by $p(\omega)$ and by differentiating (1.14) with respect to ω, we obtain:[7]

$$\frac{p'(\omega)}{p(\omega)} = \frac{1}{p(\omega)} \frac{dp(\omega)}{d(\omega)} = \frac{(k_1 - k_2)}{(\omega + k_1)(\omega + k_2)} \tag{1.15}$$

which is positive or negative, according to whether k_1 is larger or smaller than k_2. Therefore the wage–rental ratio and commodity price

Figure 1.5a

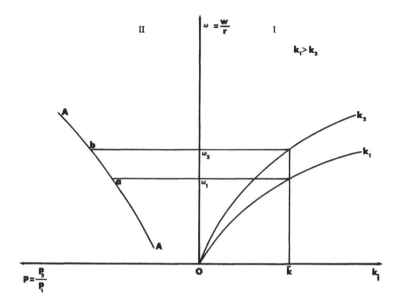

Figure 1.5b

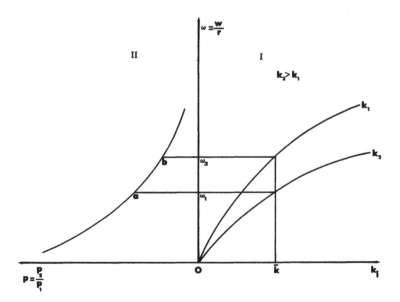

16   *A Model of a Trading World*

Figure 1.6

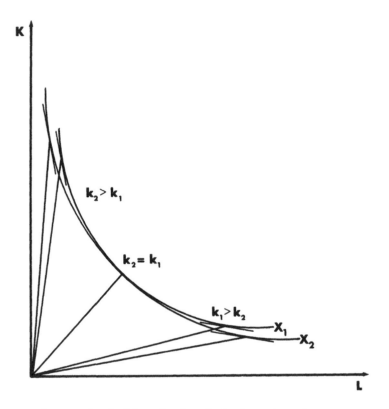

ratios are related with each other via the factor-intensity curve, as typically illustrated in Figure 1.5a and 1.5b.

The curves in Figure 1.5a and 1.5b have been drawn on the implicit assumption that there are no factor-intensity reversals. The possibility that for some ω the factor intensities may reverse themselves has not been considered. Such reversals may arise if one isoquant 'sits on the other', as illustrated in Figure 1.6. At the point at which the isoquants touch each other the factor intensities become equal to each other, while reversals occur when one compares points which lie to the left with the points to the right of the common point. The implications of factor-intensity reversals for the relationship between factor prices and commodity prices are shown in Figure 1.7. The diagram is self-explanatory. To avoid cluttering in the diagram the overall endowment condition has been omitted.

Figure 1.7

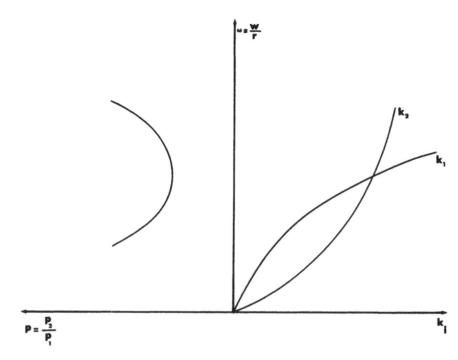

An explanation of Figure 1.5a follows. In quadrant I, the inter-relationship between the capital intensities k_i's and $\omega = w/r$, the wage-rental ratio, is represented. Given $k_1 > k_2$ an increase in the wage-rental ratio results in an increase in the capital intensity in both the sectors. This is shown by the curves k_1 and k_2. In quadrant II we present the relationship between p, the commodity price ratio, and ω, the wage-rental ratio. Given that $k_1 > k_2$, we know from equation (1.15) that this is positive. The curve AA illustrates this relationship. It is important here to draw attention to the fact that all points in Figure 1.5a are not feasible. The feasible points are obtained by imposing the full-employment condition on the model. Suppose the overall capital-labour ratio is given by $\bar{k}$. Let $O\bar{k}$ represent this ratio in Figure 1.5a. It follows immediately that the range of variation in the wage-rental ratio is then given by ω_1 and ω_2. Obviously, the economy is completely specialised in X_1 if ω_1 prevails and in X_2 if ω_2 becomes the established wage–rental ratio. The range of commodity price ratio for which the economy remains incompletely specialised is indicated by points that lie in the open interval (a, b), i.e. at points that are between a and b in quadrant II. Figure 1.5b is self-explanatory.

1.3 Production Possibility Curve

In this section we derive geometrically the production possibility curve (also known as the transformation curve). Many results in trade theory are either proved or illustrated with the help of the production possibility curve. The production possibility curve shows the various combinations of amounts of the two commodities which might be produced under competitive conditions. Given our present assumptions, it also represents the maximum possible output of one commodity given the output of the other, i.e. $X_1 = X_1(X_2)$.

The production possibility curve is generally derived with the help of the Edgeworth–Bowley box diagram, for the case in which two commodities X_1 and X_2 are competitively produced with the help of the two inelastically supplied primary factors of production labour (L) and capital (K).[8] Since the two factors of production are fixed in supply (equations 1.11, 1.12), a box can be constructed as in Figure 1.8, the dimensions of which represent the total supply of the factors of production. Outputs are measured by reference to the origins O_1 and O_2, and any point in the box reflects a certain allocation of capital and labour between the two commodities. Given our assumptions about the nature of production functions, the level of output can be measured by the distances of their isoquants from the respective origins. The diagonal O_1O_2 measures the overall capital–labour ratio. This diagram plays an important role in the derivation of the production possibility schedule. It has already been stated that each point of a particular isoquant represents the same level of output, and hence the output of each commodity can be measured by the intersection between the isoquant and the diagonal. For example, the output of the first commodity X_1, represented by isoquant x_1 and x_1', is indicated by O_1a_1 and O_1a_1' respectively. Similarly, the points O_2b_2 and O_2b_2' can be interpreted. Given these interpretations of points along the diagonal, a movement away from O_1 towards O_2 represents an increase in the output of the first commodity X_1 and a decline in the output of the second commodity X_2 and vice versa.

By introducing the Pareto optimality criterion the contract locus and the production possibility curve can be derived. This criterion states that a production point is efficient if every other feasible reallocation

Figure 1.8

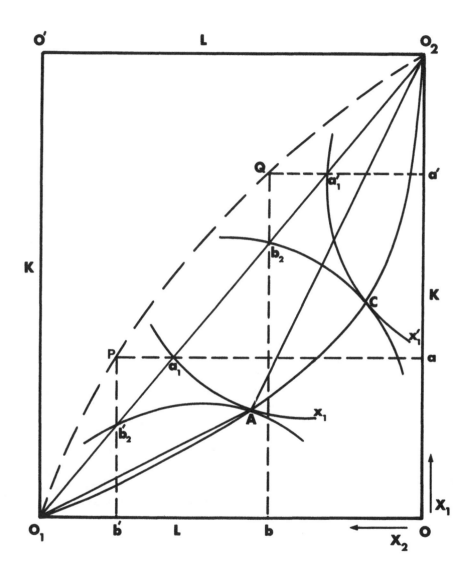

of inputs results in a decrease in the output of at least one commodity. In view of this criterion efficiency in the allocation of the two resources labour and capital can be attained at points such as A and C, where the isoquants of the two commodities are tangential to each other. The locus of all tangency points, the curve O_1ACO_2, is called the contract curve or the efficiency locus.

The position of the contract curve in the box depends on the assumption regarding the capital intensity of the two sectors. The contract curve in the diagram lies below the diagonal because of our assumption that sector 2 is capital-intensive relative to sector 1. This is clear by observing that the slope of O_1A with respect to the O_1O axis is less than the capital–labour ratio in X_2, which is given by the slope of O_2A with respect to O_2O' axis. If, instead of X_2, X_1 was the capital-intensive commodity, then the contract curve would lie entirely above the diagonal. If the capital intensities of the two sectors are identical, the diagonal in effect becomes the contract curve.

The production possibility curve can be derived from the contract curve. We have already established that various points on the diagonal represent different levels of output of each commodity. If we transform this measuring scale to the vertical and the horizontal axis with the origin O, the transformation curve can be obtained. For example, the output levels of X_1, given by points a_1 and a_1' on the diagonal, can be projected towards the OO_2 axis to points a and a' respectively. Since the production functions are assumed to be homogeneous of degree one, the distance O_1a_1' exceeds O_1a_1 in exactly the same proportion as Oa' exceeds Oa. Similarly, the output of X_2 can be projected to obtain the points on the horizontal and vertical axis.

Derivation of the points in the commodity space follows. The output associated with point A is given respectively by Oa and Ob'. The output combination given by points a and b' is then furnished by point P in the commodity space. In similar fashion the output combination at C is associated with point Q in the output space. The locus of all such points is called the production possibility curve which is given by O_1PQO_2. The production possibility curve is concave towards the origin. This is so due to our assumption of constant returns to scale, difference in the factor intensity of the two sectors and perfect competition on both sides of the market. Given constant returns to scale and the assumption of competitive markets, the economy may at worst have a straight line transformation curve. Since both industries are characterised by constant returns to scale if one industry gives up resources, the other industry can increase its output by the same proportion in which the former industry has given up the resources. Hence it is not possible to get a production possibility curve that is convex to the origin, if one assumes constant returns to scale and perfectly competitive markets.

So far we have concentrated on deriving the shape of the production possibility locus. However, we have not determined the point at which production equilibrium occurs. By differentiating equation (1.6) totally, we obtain:

$$dX_1 = \frac{\partial F_1}{\partial K_1} dK_1 + \frac{\partial F_1}{\partial L_1} dL_1$$

and

$$dX_2 = \frac{\partial F_2}{\partial K_2} dK_2 + \frac{\partial F_2}{\partial L_2} dL_2$$

From (1.8) and (1.9), we know that $r = (\partial F_1/\partial K_1) = p(\partial F_2/\partial K_2)$ and $w = (\partial F_1/\partial L_1) = p(\partial F_2/\partial L_2)$. It also follows by differentiating equations (1.11) and (1.12) that $dL_2 = -dL_1$ and $dK_2 = -dK_1$. By making appropriate substitutions, we obtain:

$$\frac{dX_1}{dX_2} = -p$$

Where dX_1/dX_2 represents the slope of the production possibility schedule and is defined as the domestic rate of transformation (DRT). The condition derived above tells us that in competitive equilibrium the slope of the production possibility curve equals the negative of the commodity price ratio.

This equilibrium condition is depicted in Figure 1.9. TT' is the production possibility curve drawn concave to the origin. The slope of the line pp represents the relative price of X_2. The equilibrium point is obtained by drawing the price line pp tangential to the production possibility curve. Thus with pp the production point is given by P where the slope of pp equals the slope of the production possibility curve. By superimposing the indifference curves of Figure 1.1 on Figure 1.9 the consumption equilibrium is obtained. In Figure 1.9 the consumption equilibrium occurs at point C, the welfare level is indicated by U, AC of commodity 2 is imported in exchange for PA of commodity 1. The triangle PAC is known as the trade triangle. In equilibrium, as is clear from the diagram, the domestic rate of substitution in consumption (DRS) equals the domestic rate of transformation (DRT) which in turn equals the foreign rate of transformation (given by the slope of pp).

Figure 1.9

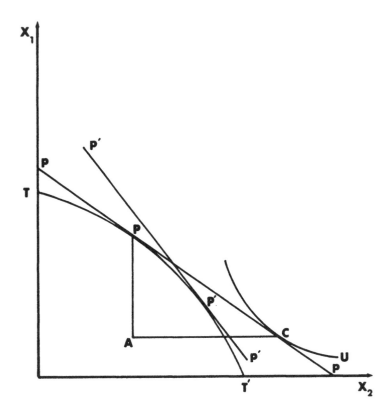

The concavity of the production possibility curve coupled with the equilibrium condition that the ratio of prices equals the domestic rate of transformation (which implies an increase in the relative price of X_2) results in an increase in the output of commodity 2. The increase in the relative price of commodity 2 is reflected by the slope of the price line $p'p'$. This price line is tangential to the production possibility curve at point P', where output of X_2 has increased while the output of X_1 has declined compared with the original equilibrium position.[9]

1.4 The Rybczynski Theorem

In this section the implications of a change in factor endowments (at constant prices) are examined for the levels of output of the two industries. Let us first consider the implications of a small increase in the capital stock K. The output response can be obtained by differentiating the production functions with respect to K. With prices held constant, it follows from equations (1.8) and (1.9) that the optimal capital—labour ratio will remain undisturbed as long as both industries have positive outputs. Hence by differentiating equation (1.7) with respect to K, we obtain:

$$\frac{dX_i}{dK} = f_i \frac{dL_i}{dK} \quad i = 1, 2 \tag{1.16}$$

and from equations (1.11) and (1.12):

$$\frac{dL_1}{dK} = -\frac{1}{(k_2 - k_1)} \tag{1.17}$$

$$\frac{dL_2}{dK} = \frac{1}{(k_2 - k_1)} \tag{1.18}$$

Substituting from equations (1.17) and (1.18) into equation (1.16):

$$\frac{dX_1}{dK} = -\frac{f_1}{(k_2 - k_1)} \tag{1.19}$$

$$\frac{dX_2}{dK} = \frac{f_2}{(k_2 - k_1)} \tag{1.20}$$

Similarly:

$$\frac{dX_1}{dL} = \frac{k_2 f_1}{(k_2 - k_1)} \tag{1.21}$$

$$\frac{dX_2}{dL} = -\frac{k_1 f_2}{(k_2 - k_1)} \tag{1.22}$$

From equation (1.19) to (1.21), the Rybczynski theorem is easily obtained:

Theorem 1.1 (Rybczynski theorem): In an incompletely specialised two-factor, two-commodity economy an increase in the endowment of any factor at constant prices results in an increase (decrease) in the output of the industry that uses the factor intensively (non-intensively).

This is a remarkable theorem, for it shows that an increase in the endowment of a factor does not lead to an increase in all outputs, but on the contrary leads to an absolute increase in the output of one industry and an absolute decline in the output of the other industry. The economic explanation of the above result can be easily appreciated by examining the following equation regarding the factor endowments:

Figure 1.10

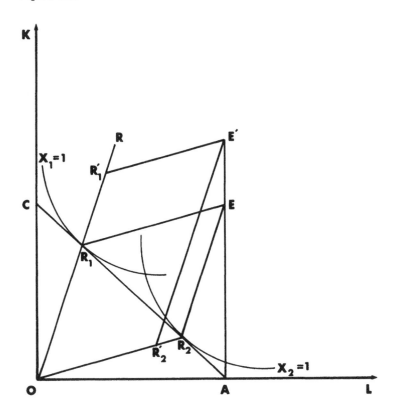

$$k_1 \frac{L_1}{\bar{L}} + k_2 \frac{L_2}{\bar{L}} = \frac{K}{\bar{L}}$$

If we suppose that K increases, this implies that the right-hand side of the above equation rises, hence the left-hand side must also rise. At constant prices k_1 and k_2 cannot change, and hence all adjustment must occur through changes in $L_1/\bar{L}$ and $L_2/\bar{L}$. Assuming $k_1 > k_2$, then the only way the left-hand side can rise is through an increase in $L_1/\bar{L}$, which implies that $L_2/\bar{L}$ must fall. It is obvious from (1.7) that a decrease in L_2 with constant k_2 implies that the output of X_2 must decline, which happens to be the sector that uses capital non-intensively.

The Rybczynski theorem can be proved geometrically either with the help of the Edgeworth–Bowley box diagram or with the help of the isoquant diagram. The Rybczynski theorem is presented geometrically with the help of the latter technique in Figure 1.10. Let us suppose that at factor prices given by the slope of the line CA, production equilibrium occurs at points R_1 and R_2 where the unit isoquants of commodities X_1 and X_2 are tangential with the line CA. The factor intensities of commodities X_1 and X_2 are indicated by the slopes of the line OR_1 and OR_2. Since X_1 is the capital-intensive commodity the slope of $OR_1 > OR_2$. Point E indicates the endowment point, i.e. the overall availability of capital and labour. The economy is assumed to be in full-employment equilibrium, hence, the vector sum of OR_1 and OR_2 coincides with point E. Let us consider the implications of an increase in the capital stock. Suppose capital stock increases from AE to AE', so that the new endowment point becomes E'. Given fixed commodity and factor prices, which imply unchanged factor intensities, the new production equilibrium must occur along the rays OR_1 and OR_2. The new production points compatible with full employment are R_1' and R_2' (isoquants have been omitted). R_1' indicates a higher output of the capital-intensive commodity X_1 and R_2' a lower output of the labour-intensive commodity X_2.

1.5 The Stolper–Samuelson Theorem

Finally in this chapter, we examine the implications of a change in the commodity prices for the factor rewards.

From the results relating to the interrelationship between commodity and factor prices, we know that an increase in the commodity price ratio results in an increase (decrease) in the wage–rental ratio if sector 1 is capital-intensive (labour-intensive) compared with sector 2. The Stolper–Samuelson theorem relates movements in commodity prices to individual rewards rather than to the ratio of factor rewards. By differentiating equations (1.8) and (1.9) logarithmically with respect to p_1 and p_2, we obtain:

$$\frac{d \log r}{d \log p_1} = -\frac{k_1 + \omega}{(k_2 - k_1)} \tag{1.23}$$

$$\frac{d \log r}{d \log p_2} = \frac{k_2 + \omega}{(k_2 - k_1)} \tag{1.24}$$

$$\frac{d \log w}{d \log p_1} = -\frac{k_2(k_1 + \omega)}{\omega(k_1 - k_2)} \tag{1.25}$$

$$\frac{d \log w}{d \log p_2} = \frac{k_1(k_2 + \omega)}{\omega(k_1 - k_2)} \tag{1.26}$$

Figure 1.11

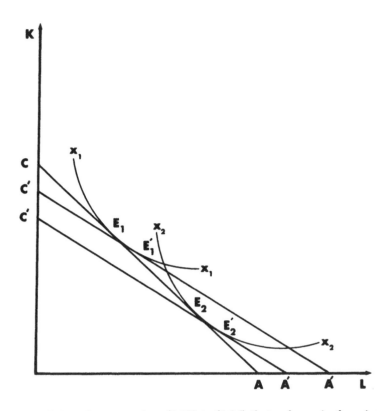

It is obvious from equations (1.23) to (1.26) that a change in the price of a commodity affects the rental on capital and the wage rate via the factor intensities of the commodities. For instance, a rise in the price of commodity 1 increases (decreases) the rental on capital (wage) depending on $k_1 \gtrless k_2$. Moreover, $d \log r/d \log p_1$ and $d \log w/d \log p_2$ are greater than one when $k_1 > k_2$. Similarly $d \log r/d \log p_2$ and $d \log w/d \log p_1$ are greater than one when $k_2 > k_1$. The Stolper–Samuelson theorem is obtained from equations (1.23) to (1.26).

Theorem 1.2 (Stolper–Samuelson theorem): In an incompletely specialised two-factor, two-commodity economy an increase (decrease) in the price of any commodity raises (lowers) the real reward of the factor used intensively (non-intensively) in the production of the commodity of which the price has increased.

The Stolper–Samuelson theorem can be demonstrated geometrically with the help of an isoquant diagram. This is done in Figure 1.11. Let the commodity units be such that the price ratio ($p_2/p_1 = 1$). This implies that the isoquants x_1x_1 and x_2x_2 are tangential to the same isocost line CA. The slope of CA gives the wage–rental ratio. Assume that commodity 1 is capital-intensive. Now suppose that the price of good 1 rises. This increase in price of good 1 implies that at the new equilibrium position the average cost of producing commodity 1 must be higher than that of commodity 2. Hence, new equilibrium occurs at points E_1' and E_2', implying that the wage–rental ratio falls. In both sectors the capital–labour ratio falls and, given our restrictions on the production functions, the marginal product of labour falls in terms of both the commodities and the marginal product of capital rises in terms of both commodities. This is indeed a remarkable result because of the way it avoids the index number problem in obtaining the impact of a change in commodity price on factor rewards.

1.6 Summary

In this chapter, we have presented the standard two-factor, two-commodity barter model of international trade and discussed its important properties. In presenting the model, certain micro-economics concepts have also been discussed in some detail. For example, we have looked at the assumptions regarding the production functions, the box diagram and the derivation and the properties of the production possibility curve. On the basis of the model the following results were established.

(1) In the absence of factor-intensity reversals there is a one-to-one relationship between factor prices and commodity prices. This one-to-one relationship depends on the physical-factor intensity ranking of the two sectors, for instance if $k_1 > k_2$ then an increase in the relative price of commodity 2 results in an increase in the wage-rental ratio. Factor-intensity reversals upset this one-to-one relationship.

(2) In competitive equilibrium the slope of the production possibility curve (DRT) equals the negative of the commodity price ratio, i.e. $dX_1/dX_2 = -p$, which in turn equals the domestic rate of substitution in consumption (DRS). Since we have made the small country assumption it follows that the competitive equilibrium is characterised by DRS = DRT = p = FRT.

(3) In an incompletely specialised two-factor, two-commodity economy an increase in the endowment of any factor at constant prices results in an increase (decrease) in the output of the industry that uses the factor intensively (non-intensively). This is known as the Rybczynski theorem.

(4) In an incompletely specialised two-factor, two-commodity economy an increase (decrease) in the price of any commodity raises (lowers) the real reward of the factor used intensively (non-intensively) in the production of the commodity of which the price has increased. This is known as the Stolper–Samuelson theorem. Results (3) and (4) are duals of each other.

Notes

1. This model is known as the Heckscher–Ohlin–Samuelson model of international trade. This particular name was given to the model by Bhagwati (2) in his survey article.

2. Most text books on the theory of international trade start with a chapter on a completely closed economy, see, for example, Batra (1). This is done partly for pedagogical reasons and partly for interest in theories of comparative advantage which determine the pattern of trade. While the determination of the pattern of trade is no doubt an important question, it is not the focus of attention in the present work. Moreover, excellent treatments are available regarding the two important theorems of comparative advantage, the Ricardian and Heckscher–Ohlin. See for example Batra (1), Bhagwati (2), (3), Caves (4), Caves and Jones (5) and Chipman (6).

3. From this equilibrium condition the stability conditions can easily be derived. These stability conditions are known as the Marshall–Lerner stability conditions. These conditions are derived in Appendix I. Throughout the present book it will be assumed that the stability conditions are satisfied.

4. The words industry, commodity and sector will be used synonymously.

5. This diagram can also be used to get an intuitive idea of the meaning of the limit conditions imposed on the production functions. For instance, the condition $\lim_{k_i \to 0} f_i'(k_i) = \infty$ states that as the capital–labour ratio approaches zero the marginal product of capital approaches infinity. This is easily seen on the diagram. The tangent at point R gives the marginal product of capital. As $k_i \to 0$ the tangent becomes steeper and in the limit approaches infinity.

6. There are, of course, other ways of closing the model, for example, assuming a single country facing a fixed foreign offer curve.

7. It is important to distinguish the function $p(\omega)$ from the international price ratio p. The model is solved as soon as p, the international price ratio, is supplied from outside in the small-country case.

8. The technique we are using for deriving the production possibility locus is known as the Savosnick (14) technique.

9. It should be pointed out here that the concavity of the locus is not a sufficient condition for the positive relationship between own price change and output movements. For instance, in the case of wage differentials perverse price

output movements can occur in spite of the concavity of the production possibility locus.

References

The Pattern of Trade

(1) Batra, R. N. 1973. *Studies in the Pure Theory of International Trade.* London: Macmillan.
(2) Bhagwati, J. N. 1964. The Pure Theory of International Trade: A Survey. *Economic Journal,* 74 (March), 1–84.
(3) Bhagwati, J. N. 1967. The Proofs of the Theorems on Comparative Advantage. *Economic Journal,* 77 (March), 75–83.
(4) Caves, R. E. 1960. *Trade and Economic Structure.* Cambridge, Mass.: Harvard University Press.
(5) Caves, R. E., and Jones, R. W. 1973. *World Trade and Payments: An Introduction.* Boston: Little, Brown.
(6) Chipman, J. S. 1965, 1966 and 1966. A Survey of the Theory of International Trade. *Econometrica,* Vol. 33 (July), 477–519; Vol. 33 (October), 685–760; and Vol. 34 (January), 18–76.

Properties of the Model

(7) Jones, R. W. 1965. The Structure of Simple General Equilibrium Model. *Journal of Political Economy,* Vol. 73 (December), 557–72.
(8) Jones, R. W. 1965. Duality in International Trade: A Geometrical Note. *Canadian Journal of Economics and Political Science,* Vol. 31 (August), 390–3.
(9) Rybczynski, T. M. 1955. Factor Endowments and Relative Commodity Prices. *Economica,* new series, Vol. 22 (November), 181–97.
(10) Stolper, W. F., and Samuelson, P. A. 1941. Protection and Real Wages. *Review of Economic Studies,* Vol. 9 (November), 58–73.

Technical Equipment

(11) Allen, R. G. D. 1938. *Mathematical Analysis for Economists.* London: Macmillan.
(12) Eisenberg, E. 1961. Aggregation of Utility Functions. *Management Science,* Vol. 7 (July), 337–50.
(13) Samuelson, P. A. 1956. Social Indifference Curves. *Quarterly Journal of Economics,* Vol. 70 (February), 1–22.
(14) Savosnick, K. M. 1958. The Box Diagram and the Production Possibility Curve. *Ekonomisk Tidskrift,* Vol. 60 (September), 183–97.

Part One

**THE THEORY OF FACTOR PRICE
DIFFERENTIALS AND THE PURE
THEORY OF INTERNATIONAL TRADE**

2 FACTOR PRICE DIFFERENTIALS, THE SHAPE OF THE TRANSFORMATION LOCUS AND THE RELATIONSHIP BETWEEN PRICES AND OUTPUT LEVELS

This part of the book (Chapters 2–5) deals with some aspects of the theory of international trade under the assumption that the factor markets are imperfect. The factor market imperfection is assumed to take a specific form, namely that a qualitatively identical factor earns a higher reward in one sector of the economy compared with its reward in the other sector of the same economy.[1] This type of factor price differential is regarded as distortionary and is distinguished from factor price differentials that need not be distortionary.[2] For example, an observed wage differential between the rural and urban sector does not represent a genuine distortion if it is caused by, say, a utility preference between occupations on the part of the wage-earners. A factor price differential is considered to be distortionary when it cannot be explained on legitimate economic grounds. Various reasons may be advanced for the presence of a distortionary factor price differential. The reasons typically given in the literature are, for instance, differential factor taxation (Harberger (3)); or trade union intervention and the existence of the wage differential between the industrial and the subsistence sector of an underdeveloped economy.[3] It is important to note that the distortionary factor price differential is assumed to exist in spite of the assumption of perfect factor mobility between sectors.

In this chapter the standard model of trade presented earlier is extended to include the presence of a factor price differential. Since there are two factors of production in the model, capital (K) and labour (L), there are two markets in which factor price differentials can be introduced. However, to keep the exposition simple, we only introduce factor price differential in one market. We introduce an exogenous distortion in the labour market in which it is assumed that the qualitatively identical factor, labour, does not earn the same reward in both sectors of the economy. Given the presence of this exogenous distortion several issues are examined in this chapter, for instance, the relationship between commodity prices and factor prices, the impact of the distortion on the shape of the production possibility locus and the relation between changes in commodity prices and levels of output.

2.1 The Model With the Factor Price Differential (Wage Differential)

The standard model presented earlier needs to be modified to accommodate the presence of a factor price differential. The wage differential is introduced in the following form:[4]

$$\mu w_1 = w_2 \quad \mu > 0, \mu \gtreqless 1 \tag{2.1}$$

where w_i ($i = 1, 2$) indicates the wages in sectors 1 and 2 and μ the differential between the two sectors. In the distortionary case μ is assumed to be positive and not equal to one. The value of μ greater than one (less than one) implies that the wage in sector 1 is lower (higher) than in sector 2. Thus the value of μ indicates the direction of the wage differential[5] and $\mu = 1$ indicates the absence of a wage differential.

The presence of the wage differential results in modification of equations relating to the reward of the factors of production. This occurs because the firms in sector 1 and 2 maximise profits subject to different wage–rental ratios. From the assumption of profit maximisation, it follows that the wages in sector 1 equal the value of their marginal product in sector 1 and similarly wages in sector 2 equal the value of their marginal product in sector 2, hence:

$$w_1 = f_1 - k_1 f_1' \tag{2.2}$$

$$w_2 = p(f_2 - k_2 f_2') \tag{2.3}$$

Therefore, by using (2.1), it follows:

$$\mu w_1 = w_2 = \mu(f_1 - k_1 f_1') = p(f_2 - k_2 f_2'), \quad \mu \neq 1 \tag{2.4}$$

The condition regarding the rental on capital remains the same as in Chapter 1. However, we obtain the following conditions for the equilibrium wage–rental ratio:

$$\frac{f_1 - k_1 f_1'}{f_1'} = \frac{w_1}{r} = \omega \tag{2.5}$$

$$\frac{f_2 - k_2 f_2'}{f_2'} = \frac{w_2}{r} = \mu\omega \tag{2.6}$$

Without any loss of generality, it is assumed that the aggregate supply of labour equals unity. This assumption is added to simplify the algebraic manipulation in the present chapter. The production functions can be written as:

$$X_1 = L_1 f_1(k_1) \tag{2.7}$$

$$X_2 = (1 - L_1)f_2(k_2) \tag{2.8}$$

The relationship between sectoral factor intensities and the aggregate capital–labour ratio may now be written as:

$$L_1k_1 + (1 - L_1)k_2 = k \tag{2.9}$$

Presented above are the equations that are modified by the introduction of the wage differential and we are in a position to derive interesting results.

2.2 Factor Intensities, Factor Prices and Commodity Prices in the Presence of the Wage Differential

In this section the following relationships are examined:

(a) the relationship between factor prices and factor intensities; and
(b) the relationship between commodity prices and factor prices in the presence of a wage differential.

Given the restriction on the production functions, it is obvious from equations (2.5) and (2.6) that k_1 and k_2 can be solved uniquely as functions of ω. Hence, by differentiating equations (2.5) and (2.6) with respect to ω the relationship between the wage–rental ratio and the sectoral capital–labour ratios can be obtained. These are given below:

$$\frac{dk_1}{d\omega} = -\frac{(f_1')^2}{f_1 f_1''} \tag{2.10}$$

$$\frac{dk_2}{d\omega} = -\frac{(f_2')^2}{f_2 f_2''} \mu \tag{2.11}$$

which are always positive in view of $f_i'' < 0$. This is the same as the relationship obtained in the non-distortionary model. Thus, the presence of a wage differential does not affect the interrelationship between capital intensities and the factor price ratio. The intuitive explanation of this result has already been given in Chapter 1.

From equation (1.8), it follows:

$$\frac{f_1'(k_1)}{f_2'(k_2)} = p \tag{2.12}$$

The left-hand side of this equation is a function of ω alone. Let this function be denoted by $p(\omega)$. By differentiating (2.12) with respect to ω and by using (2.10) and (2.11), we obtain:

$$\frac{1}{p}\frac{dp}{d\omega} = \frac{(\mu k_1 - k_2)}{(\omega + k_1)(\mu\omega + k_2)} \tag{2.13}$$

which is positive or negative, according to whether μk_1 is larger or smaller than k_2.

In the non-distortionary case ($\mu = 1$), the relationship between commodity prices and factor prices depends on $k_1 \gtrless k_2$, that is the difference between the physical factor intensities in the two industries (as shown in Chapter 1). When the economy is characterised by factor price differentials the direction of change in the above-mentioned variable depends on $\mu k_1 \gtrless k_2$, that is the difference in the value intensity of the two industries.[6]

Before offering an explanation of the result contained in equation (2.13), it is important to discuss the distinction between physical-factor intensities and value-factor intensities.[7]

2.2.1 Physical-Factor Intensities and Value-Factor Intensities

A detailed treatment of the distinction between physical intensities ($k_1 \gtrless k_2$) and value intensities ($\mu k_1 \gtrless k_2$) is now offered. Let PI represent the difference in the capital–labour ratios between sectors 1 and 2, that is,

$$PI = (k_1 - k_2) = \left[\frac{K_1}{L_1} - \frac{K_2}{(1 - L_1)} \right] \tag{2.14}$$

Value intensity can now be easily defined. The value intensity of a sector is defined to be $r_1 K_1 / w_1 L_1$, that is the ratio between the total value of capital and labour employed in a sector. Let VI represent the difference between the value intensity of the two sectors:

$$VI = \frac{r_1 K_1}{w_1 L_1} - \frac{r_2 K_2}{w_2(1 - L_1)} \tag{2.15}$$

In the absence of factor price differentials both sectors face the same rental–wage ratio, and hence

$$VI = \frac{r}{w}(k_1 - k_2) \quad \text{where } r = r_1 = r_2 \text{ and } w = w_1 = w_2 \tag{2.16}$$

It is obvious from (2.14) and (2.16) that in the non-distorted model the sign of PI and VI are identical:

Sign PI = Sign VI

Thus, if a sector is capital-intensive in the physical sense, it is also capital-intensive in the value sense. This is an intuitively obvious result because if a sector employs more capital per unit of labour relative to the other sector and both sectors face the same rental–wage ratio then the relative share of capital in the capital-intensive sector must be higher than in the labour-intensive sector.

In the presence of a wage differential the sign of PI need not be the same as the sign of VI. In other words, the ranking of sectors in the physical sense may not be the same as the ranking of sectors in the value sense. Given our assumption that $w_1 \neq w_2$, more specifically $\mu w_1 = w_2, \mu \neq 1$, VI reduces to the following expression:

$$VI = \frac{r}{w_2}(\mu k_1 - k_2) \tag{2.17}$$

Suppose that sector 1 is physically capital-intensive compared with sector 2 $(k_1 > k_2)$. However, $\mu \neq 1$. Let $\mu < 1$; then it is possible for $(\mu k_1 - k_2) < 0$, when $(k_1 - k_2) > 0$. In other words, though sector 1 is physically capital-intensive, it is labour-intensive in the value sense. This happens because when $\mu < 1$, sector 1 pays a premium to labour. Hence, each unit of labour employed in sector 1 earns a higher reward than each unit of labour employed in sector 2. The payment of a premium to labour in sector 1 naturally results in an increase in the share of labour in sector 1. This share can become so high that sector 1 may end up becoming labour-intensive in the value sense.

It should also be pointed out at this stage that the presence of a wage differential may also reverse the physical-factor intensities.[8] Furthermore, it is also possible for both intensities, i.e. physical and value, to reverse simultaneously.

These results on value-intensity reversals and physical-factor-intensity reversals can be easily presented in terms of diagrams. The case of value-intensity reversal is presented first. In Figure 2.1a, we measure capital intensity on the horizontal axis and output per unit of labour on the vertical axis. The production functions are represented by the curves $f_i(k_i)$. Sector 1 is assumed to be capital-intensive. Suppose both sectors face the same wage–rental ratio as denoted OS. From OS draw tangents to the curves $f_i(k_i)$ to obtain the equilibrium levels of k_i's, which are indicated by points OQ_2 and OQ_1. Since sector 1 is capital-intensive $OQ_1 > OQ_2$. Total output per worker in sectors 1 and 2 is indicated by OA. The share of capital per worker in sector 1 is given by AC and in sector 2 by AB. The wage bill in sector 1 equals OC and in sector 2, OB. The ratio AC/OC indicates the value intensity in sector 1. It is obvious from the diagram that the ratio AC/OC > AB/OB, that is, sector 1 is capital-intensive both in the physical as well as the value sense.

Now consider the case in which sector 1 pays a premium to labour

Figure 2.1a

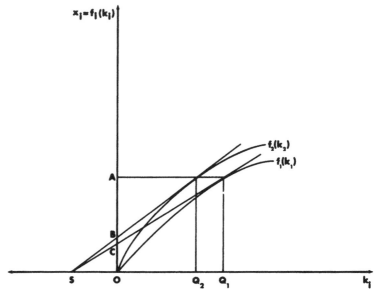

Figure 2.1b

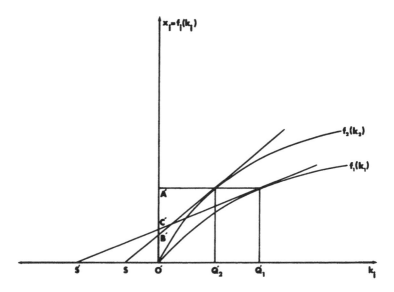

($\mu < 1$). This implies that the wage–rental ratio in sector 1 is greater than the wage–rental ratio in sector 2 ($w_1/r > w_2/r$). In Figure 2.1b, the wage–rental ratio in sector 2 is indicated by $O'S$ and in sector 1 by $O'S'$. $O'S' > O'S$ implies that sector 1 pays a premium to labour. Given the wage–rental ratios the equilibrium physical-factor intensities are indicated by points Q_1' and Q_2'. The equilibrium value of the capital intensity in sector 1, $O'Q_1'$, is greater than the corresponding value in sector 2, $O'Q_2'$. Hence, sector 1 is physically capital-intensive and sector 2 physically labour-intensive. The value intensities in the two sectors are now given by the ratios $A'C'/O'C'$ in sector 1 and by $A'B'/O'B'$ in sector 2. It is obvious from the diagram that $A'B'/O'B' > A'C'/O'C'$, implying that sector 1 is labour-intensive and sector 2 capital-intensive in value sense. In other words, the value intensities have reversed and are no longer the same as the physical intensities of the two sectors.[9]

Let us now consider the case in which sector 2 pays the premium to labour ($\mu > 1$). This implies that the wage–rental ratio in sector 2 is greater than in sector 1 ($w_2/r > w_1/r$). In Figure 2.2 the wage-rental ratio in sector 2 is indicated by OM and in sector 1 by OM'. The equilibrium values of capital intensities are indicated by k_1 and k_2 and it is obvious from the diagram that the differential has caused sector 1 to be labour-intensive compared with sector 2 ($k_2 > k_1$).

From our discussion of the reversal of value intensities and physical-factor intensities the following theorem follows.

Theorem 2.1: A necessary condition for value-intensity reversal is that the physically capital-intensive sector pays a premium to labour. The necessary condition for the reversal of physical-factor intensities is that the physically labour-intensive sector pays a premium to labour.

The distinction between physical-factor intensities and value intensities is exceedingly important in the presence of factor price differentials. The physical-factor proportions govern the relationships between the real variables of the model, for instance the commodity outputs and factor endowments. The value ranking links the value variables, for example, the prices of commodities and factor rewards. A central feature of the two-sector model of general equilibrium is that the ranking of sectors by physical and value intensity is always identical, and hence responses to parametric changes take the expected form. However, as shown in Figure 2.1b, this need not be so in the distortionary model. Once the inter-connection between the value and the

Figure 2.2

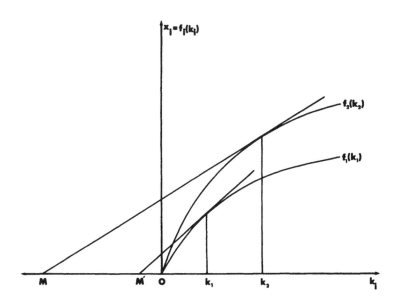

physical variables is lost, all kinds of perverse responses can arise. For example, output may respond perversely to its own price change if value intensities reverse themselves.

2.2.2 On the Explanation of the Relation Between Commodity and Factor Prices in the Presence of a Wage Differential

It is now appropriate to offer comments on equation (2.13), which shows the relationship between changes in the wage−rental ratio and the commodity price ratio. Let us suppose that $k_1 > k_2$ and $\mu > 1$, that is, the physically labour-intensive sector pays the premium to labour. In this case a rise in the wage−rental ratio results in an increase in the commodity price ratio, an increase in the relative price of commodity 2 in comparison with commodity 1. This is a standard result and is explained in Chapter 1. The physical and value intensities are identical,

Figure 2.3

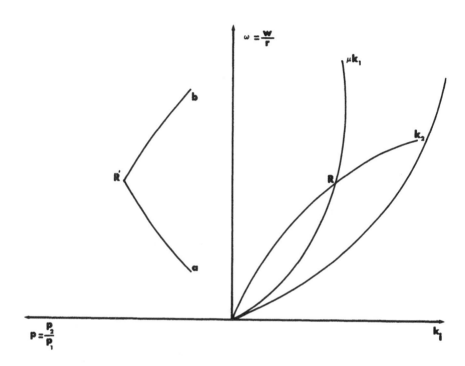

so that the standard result follows. If we suppose instead that $k_1 > k_2$, $\mu < 1$ and $\mu k_1 < k_2$, in this case an increase in the wage–rental ratio results in a fall in the price of second good relative to good one. This happens in spite of the fact that sector 2 is physically labour-intensive and sector 1 physically capital-intensive. This non-standard response is caused by value-intensity reversal. Due to value-intensity reversals sector 1 becomes labour-intensive and sector 2 capital-intensive in value sense. Hence an increase in the wage–rental ratio, with μ constant, results in an increase in the price of the commodity which is labour-intensive in the value sense. This result can be presented diagrammatically in terms of the back-to-back diagram. In Figure 2.3, value-intensity reversal occurs after point R is reached. After point R is reached the ranking of sectors in terms of the physical-factor intensities and value intensities is not the same. The relationship between ω and p is represented by curve aR'b. Before point R is reached the curve shows that an increase in ω results in an increase in the commodity price ratio (p_2/p_1). Since at point R value-intensity reversal occurs, the relationship between ω and commodity price ratio is also reversed, so p falls as ω increases. The diagram also explicitly shows the existence of multiple equilibria. Given a particular p there exist two possible wage—rental ratios; in other words, the relationship between the wage—rental ratio and the price ratio is no longer monotonic.[10]

2.3 Shrinkage and the Slope of the Production Possibility Locus

In this section we examine the impact of the wage differential on the location and the slope of the production possibility curve. The problem of the location of the production possibility curve is taken up first.

The existence of a factor price differential results in a shrinkage of the production possibility curve (except at end points where the wage constraint is not binding).[11] This is intuitively obvious and can be proved rigorously with the help of the box diagram. Commodity X_1 is assumed to be labour-intensive and X_2 capital-intensive in the physical sense in Figure 2.4a. In the non-distortionary case the contract curve is given by the locus of points at which the slopes of the isoquants of industry 1 and 2 are identical. The identity of slopes indicates that both sectors face the same wage—rental ratio. With the wage differential, however, the two sectors do not face the same wage—rental ratio, so at the points of equilibrium the marginal rates of substitution for the two factors cannot be equal between the two sectors. Their slopes differ by a definite amount determined by the wage differential. This follows from equations (2.5) and (2.6), which show:

$$\mu \left[\frac{f_1 - k_1 f_1'}{f_1'} \right] = \left[\frac{f_2 - k_2 f_2'}{f_2'} \right]$$

The bracketed expressions indicate the slope of the isoquants which are not equal at the point of equilibrium due to the presence of μ. Given the above condition, the contract curve becomes the locus of points at which the two isoquant maps intersect each other. Since production takes place at these inefficient points the distorted production possibility curve shrinks. In Figure 2.4 the distorted contract curves are indicated by dotted lines. The production possibility curves corresponding to these contract curves can be easily derived via the technique outlined in Chapter 1. An explanation for one of these

Figure 2.4a

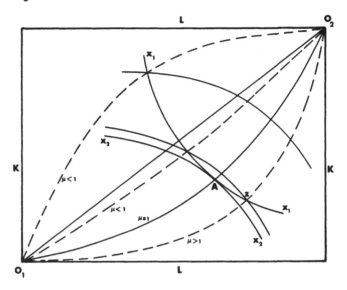

Figure 2.4b

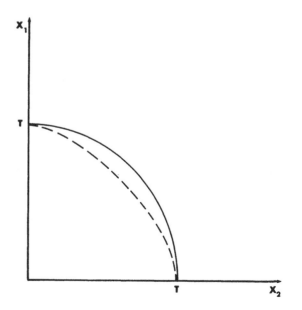

contract curves follows. Let us suppose that $\mu > 1$. This implies that sector 2, the physically capital-intensive sector, pays a premium to labour, in other words the wage–rental ratio in sector 1 is lower than the wage–rental ratio in sector 2. The distorted contract curve in this case lies below the normal contract curve O_1AO_2. It passes through a point like z, where the slope of the X_1 isoquant x_1x_1 is less than the slope of the X_2 isoquant x_2x_2, indicating that the wage–rental ratio in sector 1 is lower than in sector 2. It is only at the end points that the distorted locus coincides with the non-distorted locus, because at these points the differential is no longer a binding constraint. It should be obvious from the box diagram that the production possibility curve associated with any distorted contract curve must lie below the standard production possibility curve as illustrated in Figure 2.4b. The shrunken locus is generally called the inferior production possibility curve.

It is now appropriate to derive the slope of the production possibility curve, given μ. By differentiating the production functions totally, we obtain:

$$\frac{dX_1}{dX_2} = \frac{\dfrac{\partial X_1}{\partial L_1} dL_1 + \dfrac{\partial X_1}{\partial K_1} dK_1}{\dfrac{\partial X_2}{\partial L_2} dL_2 + \dfrac{\partial X_2}{\partial K_2} dK_2}$$

From the factor endowment conditions, it follows that $dL_1 = -dL_2$ and $dK_1 = -dK_2$. We know from the conditions on factor rewards that

$$w_1 = \frac{\partial X_1}{\partial L_1}, \quad r = \frac{\partial X_1}{\partial K_1}, \quad \frac{w_2}{p} = \frac{\partial X_2}{\partial L_2} \quad \text{and} \quad \frac{r}{p} = \frac{\partial X_2}{\partial K_2}$$

Therefore, by substitution it follows:

$$\frac{dX_1}{dX_2} = -p\beta \quad \text{where } \beta = \left[\frac{w_1 dL_1 + r dK_1}{\mu w_1 dL_1 + r dK_1}\right], \quad \beta > 0 \qquad (2.18)$$

It is obvious that $\beta \gtrless 1$ as $\mu \lessgtr 1$. Equation (2.18) clearly indicates that in the presence of distortions the slope of the production possibility locus in equilibrium does not equal the commodity price ratio. In other words, a wedge exists between the production possibility locus and the commodity price ratio (as indicated by β in equation (2.18)). Two cases of non-tangency between production possibility curve and price line are illustrated in Figures 2.5a and 2.5b. In Figure 2.5a TT' solid represents the non-distorted production possibility locus. We have already shown that the transformation locus shrinks in the presence of

Figure 2.5a

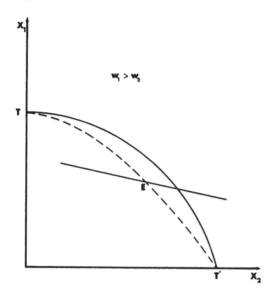

Figure 2.5b

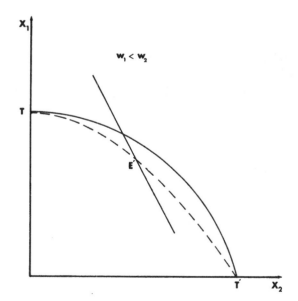

a wage differential, so the inferior transformation locus is indicated by TT' dashed (note the end points are identical). Let industry 1 pay the premium to labour ($w_1 > w_2$). This implies that $\mu < 1$, and hence in equilibrium the slope of the production possibility curve is greater than the commodity price ratio. Equilibrium occurs at a point like E where the commodity price ratio cuts the inferior production possibility curve from below. At the equilibrium point E output of X_2 is produced in a quantity greater than that which would have been produced at the optimal position. This is so because sector 2 over-expands, on account of the cheaper supply of labour compared with sector 1. Figure 2.5b shows the case in which sector 2 pays the premium to labour.

We have presented three important effects of the presence of a wage differential. These are: (1) the ranking of sectors by physical and value intensities may not be the same in the presence of a wage differential;[1][2] (2) the production possibility curve shrinks as a result of the wage differential (we have not yet discussed the shape of the inferior locus); and (3) in equilibrium the slope of the production possibility curve does not equal the commodity price ratio. The distinction between consequence (1) and (3) is exceedingly important. While (1) may exist in the presence of a wage differential (assuming incomplete specialisation), (3) always exists as a result of the wage differential provided the economy is incompletely specialised.

2.4 The Relationship Between Changes in the Relative Prices and Output Levels

This section examines the relation between a change in the commodity price ratio and the level of equilibrium outputs. To obtain an expression for this change, we first differentiate the production functions with respect to ω:

$$\frac{dX_1}{d\omega} = \frac{dL_1}{d\omega} f_1 + L_1 f_1' \frac{dk_1}{d\omega}$$

$$\frac{dX_2}{d\omega} = -\frac{dL_1}{d\omega} f_2 + (1 - L_1) f_2' \frac{dk_2}{d\omega}$$

From the factor endowment condition:

$$\frac{dL_1}{d\omega} = \frac{(k_2 - k)\left(\dfrac{dk_1}{d\omega}\right) + (k - k_1)\left(\dfrac{dk_2}{d\omega}\right)}{(k_2 - k_1)^2}$$

Therefore:

$$\frac{dX_1}{d\omega} = \frac{f_1' \left\{ (\omega + k_2)(k_2 - k)\frac{dk_1}{d\omega} + (\omega + k_1)(k - k_1)\frac{dk_2}{d\omega} \right\}}{(k_2 - k_1)^2}$$

$$\frac{dX_2}{d\omega} = \frac{f_2' \left\{ (\mu\omega + k_2)(k_2 - k)\frac{dk_1}{d\omega} + (\mu\omega + k_1)(k - k_1)\frac{dk_2}{d\omega} \right\}}{(k_2 - k_1)^2}$$

We already know that:

$$\frac{dk_1}{d\omega} = \frac{-(f_1')^2}{f_1'' f_1} \quad \text{and} \quad \frac{dk_2}{d\omega} = \frac{-(f_2')^2 \mu}{f_2'' f_2}$$

Let $\sigma(k_i)$ denote the elasticity of substitution of the factors of production of the ith commodity:[1][3]

$$\sigma(k_i) = -\frac{f_i'(f_i - k_i f_i')}{k_i f_i f_i''} > 0$$

By using the definition of elasticity of substitution, expressions for $dk_i/d\omega$ and equations (2.5) and (2.6):

$$\frac{dX_1}{d\omega} = \frac{f_1' \{(\omega + k_2)(k_2 - k)\sigma_1 k_1 + (\omega + k_1)(k - k_1)\sigma_2 k_2\}}{\omega(k_2 - k_1)^2} \qquad (2.19)$$

$$\frac{dX_2}{d\omega} = -\frac{f_2' \{(\mu\omega + k_2)(k_2 - k)\sigma_1 k_1 + (\mu\omega + k_1)(k - k_1)\sigma_2 k_2\}}{\omega(k_2 - k_1)^2} \qquad (2.20)$$

On the basis of equation (2.20) the response of the equilibrium output X_2 of the second commodity to a change in the commodity price ratio $p = (p_2/p_1)$ can be easily examined. From (2.20) it is obvious that $dX_2/d\omega \lessgtr 0$ according as $k_2 \gtrless k_1$. This inequality implies that a change in the wage—rental ratio results in a decrease, no change or an increase in the output of commodity 2, depending on whether commodity 2 is more, equal or less capital-intensive than commodity 1. To obtain the response of X_2 with respect to p the following equation needs to be evaluated:

$$\frac{dX_2}{dp} = \frac{dX_2}{d\omega} \cdot \frac{d\omega}{dp} \qquad (2.21)$$

$d\omega/dp$ has the same sign as $dp/d\omega$ in equation (2.13) and depends on value intensity. The response of equilibrium output of commodity 2 depends on two terms, one that depends on physical-factor intensity

$(dX_2/d\omega)$ and the other that depends on value-factor intensity $(d\omega/dp)$. As noted earlier, these two intensities in the wage differential framework need not have identical signs, and hence there exist a number of cases that follow from equation (2.13). Some of these cases (including the non-distortionary case) are listed below:

(1) Suppose $\mu = 1$ (non-distortionary situation). Let $k_2 > k_1$. If $k_2 > k_1$, then $(dX_2/d\omega) < 0$ and also $(dp/d\omega) < 0$. Hence, $(dX_2/dp) > 0$, implying that an increase in the relative price of X_2 results in an increase in the output of X_2.

(2) Suppose $\mu < 1$ $(w_1 > w_2)$. Let $k_2 > k_1$. These conditions imply that the physically labour-intensive sector pays the premium to labour, hence value-intensity reversals cannot occur. Given the above restrictions both $(dX_2/d\omega)$ and $(dp/d\omega)$ are negative, hence $(dX_2/dp) > 0$. In this case again the normal output price response follows.

(3) Suppose $\mu > 1$ $(w_2 > w_1)$. Let $k_2 > k_1$ but $\mu k_1 - k_2 > 0$. These conditions imply that the capital-intensive sector pays the premium to labour. The payment of this premium results in a reversal of value intensities, so the physically capital-intensive sector becomes the labour-intensive sector in the value sense. If $k_2 > k_1$ and $\mu k_1 - k_2 > 0$, then $(dX_2/d\omega) < 0$ and $(d\omega/dp) > 0$. Hence, it follows that $(dX_2/dp) < 0$.

Thus, we obtain the perverse result that an increase in the relative price of commodity 2 results in a decline in the output of the second commodity.[14] This perverse result is due to value-intensity reversal. The intuitive explanation of this result runs along the following lines. Let us suppose that given $k_2 > k_1$ value-intensity reversal has occurred, $(\mu k_1 > k_2)$, i.e. sector 2 is physically capital-intensive but labour-intensive in value sense. Now suppose that the relative price of commodity 2 increases. From equation (2.13), we know that an increase in p (given value-intensity reversal) results in an increase in the wage–rental ratio. The increase in the wage–rental ratio causes the substitution of capital for labour in both industries resulting in an excess supply of labour. It follows from the Rybczynski theorem that the excess in the supply of labour leads to an increase in the physically labour-intensive commodity and a decline in the physically capital-intensive commodity. In our case the physically labour-intensive commodity happens to be X_1, the relative price of which has fallen and the physically capital-intensive commodity X_2, the relative price of which has risen. We can now formulate the following theorem:

Theorem 2.2: Given non-reversal of physical-factor intensities a necessary condition for the perverse response of equilibrium output to an increase in its own price is value-intensity reversal.

It may be added here that if both physical- and value-factor intensities reverse only once, then normal response immediately follows.

2.5 The Shape of the Production Possibility Curve

We have just noted the possibility that equilibrium outputs may respond perversely to changes in commodity prices, an increase in price being associated with a reduction in output. A related area which has drawn considerable attention is the question of the shape of the production possibility curve and its relation with the output price response. It is now well known that in the presence of a differential the inferior production possibility curve may have any shape, that is (a) may remain concave to the origin, (b) may become convex to the origin, or (c) partly concave and partly convex to the origin, as illustrated in Figures 2.6a, 2.6b and 2.6c. The algebra needed to prove these results is highly complex, so its presentation has been omitted.[15]

An important observation that needs to be made here is that the price output relationship may be normal (abnormal) or conventional (perverse) even when the locus of competitive outputs is unconventionally (conventionally) convex (concave) to the origin. We may be sure, therefore, that circumstances exist in which the price output relationship is perverse, even though the production possibility locus is concave to the origin. Throughout this part of the book we shall assume the locus to be concave despite the presence of a differential. This assumption helps one in manipulating the model and in no way affects the validity of results presented in Chapters 2–5.

2.6 Summary

In this chapter the fully competitive model presented earlier was modified to include a factor price differential, specifically a distortionary wage differential between sectors. Given the presence of this differential, we examined the relationship between factor prices and commodity prices, the relationship between product price changes and equilibrium outputs and the shape and slope of the production possibility curve. We arrived at the following conclusions:

Figure 2.6a

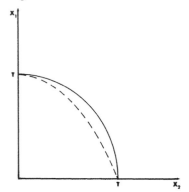

Figure 2.6b

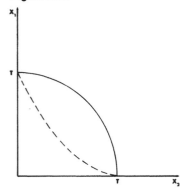

Figure 2.6c

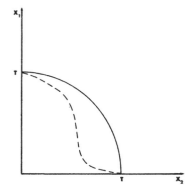

(1) In the wage differential framework it is important to distinguish physical-factor intensities from value-factor intensities. Both these intensities have the same sign in the first best framework. However, in the wage differential framework this ranking need not be the same. The absence of identical rankings is the source of several perverse results.

(2) The one-to-one correspondence between factor prices and commodity prices breaks down in the wage differential framework.

(3) The distorted production possibility curve lies inside the normal production possibility curve (except at end points) and can be of any shape.

(4) At the point of equilibrium the commodity price ratio is not tangential to the inferior transformation locus.

(5) An increase in the price of a commodity does not necessarily result in an increase in the output of the commodity of which the price has increased. In fact it may result in a fall in the output of the commodity in question. Such a perverse result is caused by value-intensity reversals.

This chapter has been mainly concerned with some of the positive aspects of the implications of wage differentials for the standard trade model. The following chapter is devoted to the normative aspects, specifically the examination of the gains from trade theorems in the presence of a distortionary factor price differential.

Notes

1. The consequences for trade theory of the existence of this type of differential has been the subject of extensive exploration in recent years. Even though some of the implications of this type of distortion were discussed by M. Manoliseco in *The Theory of Protection and International Trade* (London, P. S. King, 1935), the vast bulk of the literature has been produced in the sixties and seventies.
2. This distinction has been drawn in the well-known papers by Bhagwati and Ramaswami (1) and Bhagwati (2).
3. Other reasons for the existence of this type of distortion can be found in Bhagwati and Ramaswami (1) and Magee (4).
4. Following the general practice of literature on trade and distortions the wage differential is assumed to be a proportional difference. A constant absolute difference is a more realistic assumption to make. However, it is mathematically

difficult to handle, hence the use of a proportional difference.

5. Generally in the literature dealing with the theory of wage differentials and trade, the differential is taken to be exogenously fixed and all prices are assumed to be perfectly flexible. A paper that departs from this tradition and allows for interaction between the parameters of the model and the exogenously given wage differential is Hazari (15). This paper takes the initial position to be one of disequilibrium and suggests a mechanism that takes the system to a position of equilibrium. A certain amount of scepticism about the nature of wage differential assumed in trade theory was also expressed in a footnote in the classic paper by Bhagwati and Ramaswami (1).

6. The term value intensity was introduced in a paper by Jones (7).

7. The importance of the physical-value distinction for the entire system is explored by Jones (7).

8. Johnson (12) was the first economist to demonstrate that a wage differential may result in the reversal of the physical-factor intensities, even though in the absence of the differential the factor intensities are non-reversible.

9. This type of factor-intensity reversal should be distinguished from the traditional notion of factor-intensity reversal. The traditional factor-intensity reversal arises when one isoquant 'sits on the other'.

10. The non-monotonicity of the relationship between wage—rental ratio and the price ratio also leads to a breakdown of the factor price equalisation theorem (see Bhagwati and Srinivasan (8)). This theorem has not been discussed in the present work.

11. Shrinkage does not occur if the input coefficients are assumed to be of a fixed type (see Manning and Sgro (14)).

12. While in the two-commodity trade model value-intensity reversal explains many perverse results, this is not the case in the non-traded goods framework. The role of value-intensity reversals is of less significance in more general models (see Hazari and Sgro (5) and Hazari and Pattanaik (6)).

13. A good treatment of the concept of elasticity of substitution is available in Allen (16).

14. In many less-developed countries econometric studies show that the output of the rural sector responds perversely to price change. This result may be caused by the presence of factor price differentials, hence it might be interesting to set up econometric models that are based on imperfect factor markets.

15. See papers by Bhagwati and Srinivasan (8), Herberg and Kemp (11) and Jones (7).

References

On the Causes of Factor Price Differentials and the Distinction Between Distortionary and Non-Distortionary Factor Price Differentials

(1) Bhagwati, J. N., and Ramaswami, V. K. 1963. Domestic Distortions, Tariffs and the Theory of Optimum Subsidy. *Journal of Political Economy*, Vol. 71 (February), 44—50.

(2) Bhagwati, J. N. 1971. The Generalized Theory of Distortions and Welfare. In J. N. Bhagwati, R. W. Jones, R. Mundell and J. Vanek (eds.), *Trade, Balance of Payments and Growth*. Papers in International Economics in Honour of Charles P. Kindleberger. Amsterdam: North Holland.

(3) Harberger, A. C. 1962. The Incidence of the Corporation Income Tax. *Journal of Political Economy*, Vol. 70 (June), 215—40.

(4) Magee, S. P. 1973. Factor Market Distortions, Production and Trade: A Survey. *Oxford Economic Papers*, Vol. 25 (March), 1—43.

On the Distinction Between Physical-Factor Intensities and Value-Factor Intensities

(5) Hazari, B. R., and Sgro, P. M. 1976. Some Notes on Technical Progress in the Framework of Factor Market Imperfections and Non-Traded Goods. *Australian Economic Papers*, Vol. 16 (June), 78–86.

(6) Hazari, B. R., and Pattanaik, P. K. Some Welfare Propositions in a Three Commodity Three Factor Model of Trade. Mimeographed.

(7) Jones, R. W. 1971. Distortions in Factor Markets and the General Equilibrium Model of Production. *Journal of Political Economy*, Vol. 79 (May/June), 437–59.

On the Shape of the Transformation Locus and the Relationship Between Prices and Output Levels

(8) Bhagwati, J. N., and Srinivasan, T. N. 1971. The Theory of Wage Differentials: Production Response and Factor Price Equalisation. *Journal of International Economics*, Vol. 1 (February), 19–35.

(9) Fishlow, A., and David, P. 1961. Optimal Resource Allocation in an Imperfect Market Setting. *Journal of Political Economy*, Vol. 69 (December), 529–46.

(10) Hagen, E. 1958. An Economic Justification of Protectionism. *Quarterly Journal of Economics*, Vol. 72 (November), 496–514.

(11) Herberg, H., and Kemp, M. C. 1971. Factor Market Distortions, the Shape of the Locus of Competitive Outputs and the Relation Between Product Prices and Equilibrium Outputs. In J. Bhagwati, R. W. Jones, R. Mundell and J. Vanek (eds.), *Trade, Balance of Payments and Growth*. Papers in International Economics in Honour of Charles P. Kindleberger. Amsterdam: North Holland.

(12) Johnson, H. G. 1966. Factor Market Distortions and the Shape of the Transformation Curve. *Econometrica*, Vol. 34 (July), 686–98.

(13) Lloyd, P. J. 1970. The Shape of the Transformation Curve with and without Factor Market Distortions. *Australian Economic Papers*, Vol. 9 (June), 52–61.

(14) Manning, R., and Sgro, P. M. 1975. Wage Differentials and Growth in Fixed Coefficient Models. *Southern Economic Journal*, Vol. 41 (January), 403–9.

Also consult (7).

On a Vanishing Wage Differential

(15) Hazari, B. R. The Theory of Wage Differentials, Induced Technical Progress and the Pure Theory of International Trade. Forthcoming *Weltwirtschaftliches Archiv*.

On the Elasticity of Substitution

(16) Allen, R. G. D. 1938. *Mathematical Analysis for Economists*. London: Macmillan.

3 FACTOR PRICE DIFFERENTIALS AND THE THEOREMS ON GAINS FROM TRADE

Economists have always been interested in the welfare consequences of international trade and commercial policy. David Ricardo (12) was probably the first economist to present a formal model of trade, which could be construed in two ways: (a) as a highly simplified model demonstrating the welfare-wise superiority of free trade over no trade, or (b) as an attempt at explaining the pattern of trade. Earlier on, Smith's attack on the mercantilist doctrine of protection was based on advantages from division of labour and specialisation via international trade.

The welfare ranking of various commercial policies is not an easy task. The difficulty arises due to changes in the distribution in income associated with any change in policy. For example, a movement from a position of no trade to free trade results in a change in the distribution of income. Some people become better off by the introduction of free trade while others become worse off. In what sense then can one assert that the country as a whole benefits from the introduction of free trade? One way of making such a judgement can of course be interpersonal comparisons of utility. However, such a comparison, though intuitively appealing, is not ethically very attractive. No totally satisfactory way has so far been found to get around the difficulty of taking account of changes in the distribution of income consequent upon changes in the commercial policy.

A device which is often used to get over the problem of income distribution changes is the compensation principle. Given certain assumptions regarding technology, market structure, etc., it is possible to show, for example, that free trade is better than no trade, in the sense that there exists some system of lump-sum transfers from the gainers to losers such that every individual's position could be improved from that of no trade.[1] One serious drawback of this principle is that the compensation actually does not take place. To evaluate commercial policy, we shall use the utility function presented in Chapter 1. The existence of this utility function takes into account the welfare judgement about the income distribution.

In this chapter, the gains from trade theorems are examined under the assumption that the economy is characterised by factor price differentials. The theorems examined are: (1) free trade is better than no trade; (2) a deterioration (improvement) in the terms of trade lowers (raises) welfare; and (3) the welfare ranking of a higher versus a lower tariff.[2] The optimal commercial policy designed to correct distortions is also discussed.

3.1 The Model With Two Factor Price Differentials

The theorems on gains from trade are discussed under the assumption that both markets and/or one market is imperfect, in the sense that a qualitatively identical factor does not earn the same reward in both sectors of the economy. A wage differential was introduced in the previous chapter. A differential is now introduced in the capital market also. Since this is the most general framework, the results associated with the standard and the one-factor price differential model can be derived as a subset of the present model. Our motivation in introducing two differentials instead of one is to show the difference that multiple distortions make to results that are obtained on the basis of one differential only. The distortion in the market for capital is introduced in the following form:

$$\alpha r_1 = r_2 \quad \alpha > 0, \alpha \gtrless 1 \tag{3.1}$$

where r_i $(i = 1, 2)$ indicates the rental on capital in sectors 1 and 2 and α the differential between two sectors. In the distortionary case α is assumed to be positive and not equal to one. The value of α greater than one (less than one) implies that the rental on capital in sector 1 is lower (higher) than in sector 2. Thus the value of α indicates the direction of the rental differential and when $\alpha = 1$ capital market is not distorted.

The introduction of the rental differential leads to the following conditions regarding the reward of capital. This happens because the firms in sectors 1 and 2 maximise profits subject to different rental constraint. From the assumption of profit maximisation, it follows that the rental in sector 1 equals the value of its marginal product in sector 1 and similarly rental in sector 2 equals the value of its marginal product in sector 2, and hence:

$$r_1 = f_1' \tag{3.2}$$

$$r_2 = pf_2' \tag{3.3}$$

Therefore, by using (3.1), it follows:

$$\alpha r_1 = r_2 = \alpha f_1' = pf_2' \tag{3.4}$$

The marginal product conditions for the wages of labour remain the same as in Chapter 2. However, the following conditions hold regarding the equilibrium wage–rental ratio:

$$\frac{f_1 - k_1 f_1'}{f_1'} = \frac{w_1}{r_1} = \omega \tag{3.5}$$

$$\frac{f_2 - k_2 f_2'}{f_2'} = \frac{w_2}{r_2} = \frac{u}{\alpha} \quad \frac{w_1}{r_1} = \frac{u}{\alpha} \omega \tag{3.6}$$

We have presented the modifications needed in the model due to the introduction of two factor price differentials and are in a position to discuss the theorems on gains from trade.

3.2 Free Trade versus No Trade

In this section the proposition that under the first best assumptions free trade is better than no trade is examined.

Free trade is defined as a situation in which the international price of commodities is the same as the domestic price of the commodities. In other words, there is no difference between local prices of commodities and the international or world price of the commodities. In order to prove the optimality or otherwise of free trade, we examine the expression for change in welfare given the initial position of free trade. If this change in welfare is not equal to zero then an increase in welfare can be obtained by the choice of an appropriate policy. On the other hand, if the change in welfare equals zero then free trade is the optimal policy (the second-order conditions are assumed to be satisfied).

Differentiating (1.1) totally, we obtain:

$$dU = U_1 dD_1 + U_2 dD_2$$

or

$$\frac{dU}{U_1} = dD_1 + \frac{U_2}{U_1} dD_2 = dD_1 + p dD_2 \tag{3.7}$$

The balance of payments condition can also be expressed as stating that in equilibrium the value of production in terms of the first commodity equals the value of consumption in terms of the first commodity:[3]

$$X_1 + p X_2 = D_1 + p D_2 \tag{3.8}$$

By differentiating equation (3.8) totally (assuming the country to be small), we obtain:

$$dX_1 + pdX_2 = dD_1 + pdD_2 \qquad (3.9)$$

By substituting (3.9) in (3.7):

$$\frac{dU}{U_1} = dX_1 + pdX_2 \qquad (3.10)$$

In order to evaluate (3.10) an expression is needed for $dX_1 + pdX_2$. This can be obtained from the expression relating to the slope of the production possibility curve. By following the procedure outlined in chapter 2, the slope of the production possibility curve, given μ and α is:

$$\frac{dX_1}{dX_2} = -p\delta \quad \text{where } \delta = \left[\frac{w_1 dL_1 + r_1 dK_1}{\mu w_1 dL_1 + \alpha r_1 dK_1} \right] > 0 \qquad (3.11)$$

There exist three possible values for δ in equation (3.11): $\delta = 1$, $\delta < 1$, and $\delta > 1$. All the combinations of μ and α that give the above values of δ are listed below.

Case 1. $\delta = 1$
(a) Non-distortionary $\mu = \alpha = 1$.
(b) $\mu \gtreqless 1$ and $\alpha \lesseqgtr 1$.

In case (b) δ may equal unity if the two distortions work in opposite directions and offset each other.

Case 2. $\delta < 1$
(a) $\mu > 1, \alpha > 1$; it is obvious in this case that $\delta < 1$.
(b) $\mu \gtreqless 1$ and $\alpha \lesseqgtr 1$ and such that $\mu w_1 dL_1 + \alpha r_1 dK_1 > w_1 dL_1 + r_1 dK_1$

Case 3. $\delta > 1$
(a) $\mu < 1, \alpha < 1$, it is obvious that $\delta > 1$.
(b) $\mu \gtreqless 1$ and $\alpha \lesseqgtr 1$ and such that $\mu w_1 dL_1 + \alpha r_1 dK_1 < w_1 dL_1 + r_1 dK_1$.

Cases 1, 2 and 3 provide an interesting and exhaustive set of possibilities regarding the relationship between the slope of the production possibility curve and the commodity price ratio. We shall concentrate only on the combination of distortions that are interesting from the point of view of theorems on gains from trade.

Let us take our point of departure to be the first best case, i.e. $\mu = \alpha = 1$ and $\delta = 1$. In this case:

$$\frac{dX_1}{dX_2} = -p \qquad (3.12)$$

Figure 3.1

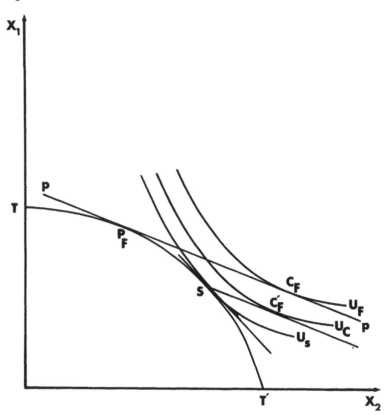

By using (3.12), (3.10) can be reduced to:

$$dU = U_1(-pdX_2 + pdX_2) = 0 \qquad (3.13)$$

$dU = 0$ clearly indicates that under the first best assumptions free trade is the optimal policy (given that the second-order conditions are satisfied).

This result can be presented geometrically. In Figure 3.1 the optimality of the free-trade policy is shown geometrically. TT′ is the production possibility curve. Pre-trade equilibrium occurs at a point where the slope of the social indifference curve is identical with the slope of the production possibility locus. Pre-trade equilibrium cannot occur at any other point because at other points the local markets will not be cleared. Thus, pre-trade equilibrium in Figure 3.1 is established at point S with welfare level U_s. Let the economy be allowed to trade at the exogenously given price ratio indicated by the slope of line pp. Since the country is assumed to be small, pp becomes the domestic price ratio. Hence, producers maximise profits and consumers utility subject to this international price ratio. Profit maximisation leads producers to produce at P_F and consumers to consume at C_F. Welfare is indicated by U_F which is greater than the welfare level associated with the no-trade position U_s. The movement from U_s to U_F (the gain in welfare) can be split up in two parts, gain due to consumption change and gain due to a production change.[4] Suppose we hold the production point constant and allow consumers to consume at the international price ratio. This would take the consumers to C'_F on the indifference curve U_C which is higher than U_s. Hence, the movement from U_s to U_C is termed the consumption gain. The rest of the gain from trade is termed the production gain.

The following theorem may now be formulated.

Theorem 3.1: Under the first best assumptions, free trade is the optimal policy. At the point of equilibrium all the rates of transformation are equal, i.e. DRS = DRT = FRT, where DRS denotes the domestic rate of substitution in consumption, DRT the domestic rate of transformation in production and FRT the foreign rate of transformation.

This theorem is now examined in the presence of factor price differentials. We first take up the case in which $\delta \neq 1$. If $\delta \neq 1$ then by substituting (3.11) in (3.10):

$$dU = U_1(1 - \delta)pdX_2 \qquad (3.14)$$

It is obvious from (3.14) that if $\delta \neq 1$ then $dU \neq 0$, so free trade is not the optimal policy in the presence of factor price differentials.

The suboptimality of the *laissez-faire* policy in the presence of factor price differentials can also be easily demonstrated geometrically. This is done in Figures 3.2a and 3.2b. In Figure 3.2a TT' indicates the inferior transformation locus. Let $\delta < 1$; hence, at the point of equilibrium the slope of the production possibility curve is less than the price ratio. Domestic production and consumption equilibrium occurs at point S and welfare level is indicated by U_0. Let the slope of P_fP_f indicate the exogenously given international price ratio. The price line P_fP_f is flatter than P_dP_d – in other words the price of X_2 relative to X_1 has decreased. Assuming a non-perverse price output response producers now produce at point P_F, the consumers consume at point C_F and the welfare level

Figure 3.2a

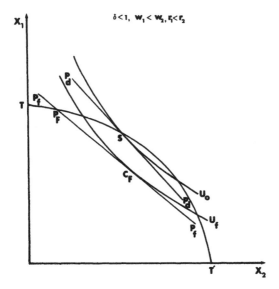

Figure 3.2b

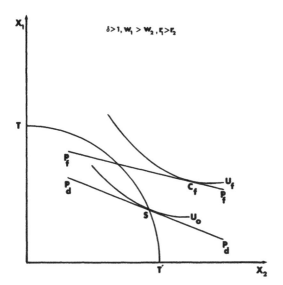

U_f is attained. Two observations need to be made regarding the free-trade equilibrium point. First, the free-trade equilibrium point is suboptimal in the sense that at the equilibrium point all the marginal rates of transformation are not equal (this is also true of the self-sufficiency situation). Second, in Figure 3.2a free trade is worse than no trade. This may or may not happen (free trade is better than no trade in Figure 3.2b).

The economic explanation of the result in Figure 3.2a is the following. Consider the case where both the differentials operate against the X_2 industry, i.e. $w_2 > w_1$ and $r_2 > r_1$. International price ratio compared with the autarky price ratio favours the X_1 sector. It is obvious from Figure 3.2a that if production is held constant at S, then the welfare will rise due to the consumption gain associated with the opening of trade. However, increased production of X_1 as indicated by point P_F results in a production loss. This happens because factors move from X_2 to X_1, which is the lower productivity sector ($w_1 < w_2$, $r_1 < r_2$), imposing a productivity loss to the economy. The production loss is greater than the consumption gain in Figure 3.2a, so that free trade turns out to be worse than autarky.

Theorem 3.2: In the presence of factor price differentials free trade is not the optimal policy.

Theorem 3.2 raises the interesting question regarding the optimal policy in the presence of factor price differentials. Before discussing the policy issue, we would like to present two lemmas regarding the equilibrium conditions under free trade in the presence of factor price differentials.

Lemma 3.1: If both labour and the capital market are distorted in the sense that there are inter-industry factor price differentials, there exist cases in which the first-order conditions are satisfied on the inferior transformation locus, that is, DRT = DRS = FRT (inferior locus).

This may happen if the two[5] distortions work in the opposite direction and the degree of distortion in one market exactly offsets the degree of distortion in the other market. It is known that factor price differentials lead to two consequences: (1) the commodity price ratio intersects the production possibility locus; and (2) the production transformation locus bows in (in extreme cases becomes convex to the origin). This proposition shows that two distortions that work in the

Figure 3.3

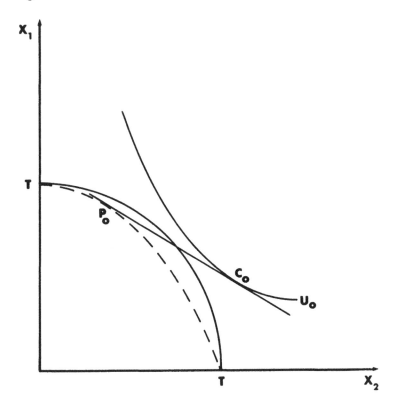

opposite directions may lead to a situation in which the tangency condition is satisfied on the inferior locus. The locus remains inferior because the distortions are not removed from the system and they affect the marginal rates of factor substitution between the industries as shown by equations (3.5) and (3.6). We present the proposition diagrammatically in Figure 3.3. TT (smooth) is the transformation locus in the case of no distortions and TT (dashed) the transformation locus in the presence of distortions. If there are two distortions offsetting each other, then the price line is tangential to the inferior locus, point P_0 on the dashed production possibility locus. Indifference curve U_0 touches the price line at C_0, thus DRS = DRT = FRT on the shrunken transformation locus.

Lemma 3.2: If the degree of distortion in both the markets is the same, that is $u = \alpha \neq 1$, then the transformation locus does not bow in, because the marginal rates of factor substitution are the same in both the sectors (see equations (3.5) and (3.6)). However, from equation (3.11) it is obvious that the domestic rate of substitution will not equal the ratio of commodity prices and a non-tangency solution will exist on the normal production transformation locus.

This result is interesting because it affects the ranking of first and second best policies. In Figure 3.4, this proposition is presented diagrammatically. TT (smooth) is the normal transformation locus and TT (broken) the inferior transformation locus. If the degree of two distortions is the same then the economy operates at the production

Figure 3.4

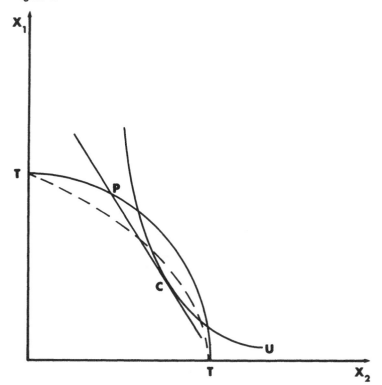

point P on the normal transformation locus and consumes at point C on
the indifference curve U.

We now return to the discussion of optimal policy. To obtain an
optimum solution one has to consider both the first-order conditions as
well as the shrinkage of the transformation curve. The first-order
conditions in our case relate to the satisfaction of equality among all
the marginal rates of transformation, i.e. DRS = DRT = FRT. To satisfy
first-order conditions for a maximum dU = 0. Suppose $\delta \neq 1$, then

$$dU = U_1 p(1 - \delta)dX_2$$

Now $dU > 0$ requires that $dX_2 \gtrless 0$ if $\delta \lessgtr 1$. Output of X_2 can be
increased or decreased by a production tax-cum-subsidy policy.

Figure 3.5

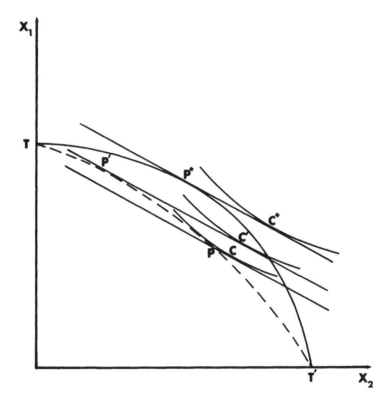

However, such a tax-cum-subsidy policy does not lead to a first best solution because it does not lead to the removal of the factor price differentials which cause the economy to operate on the inferior production possibility locus. This result is presented diagrammatically in Figure 3.5 where TT' dashed is the inferior production possibility locus. Equilibrium in production occurs at point P and in consumption at point C. A production tax-cum-subsidy policy takes the economy to points P' and C' on the inferior locus. The first best solution is given by a factor tax-cum-subsidy policy which eliminates the distortion taking the economy to production equilibrium at P'' and consumption equilibrium at C''.

Lemmas (3.1) and (3.2) give rise to two interesting results. First, if the distortions are mutually offsetting then all the theorems on gains from trade hold on the inferior production possibility locus. This happens because mutually offsetting distortions lead to the satisfaction of the first-order conditions on the inferior locus, and hence any perversities of results associated with the non-tangency between the production possibility locus and price line vanish. Second, if the two differentials are equal ($\mu = \alpha \neq 1$), then the distinction between a production tax-cum-subsidy policy and a factor tax-cum-subsidy policy ceases to exist. Both policies lead to a first best solution.[6]

3.3 Terms of Trade and Welfare

We proceed to discuss the implications of factor market imperfections for the proposition that for a small country a deterioration (improvement) in the terms of trade lowers (raises) welfare. We shall assume that only the labour market is distorted, in other words $\alpha = 1$.

By differentiating the utility function (1.1) with respect to p and suitably arranging terms:

$$\frac{1}{U_1} \frac{dU}{dp} = \frac{dD_1}{dp} + p \frac{dD_2}{dp} \tag{3.15}$$

By differentiating equations (1.3), (1.4) and (1.5) with respect to p and substituting, equation (3.15) can be transformed to:

$$\frac{1}{U_1} \frac{dU}{dp} = \frac{dX_1}{dp} + p \frac{dX_2}{dp} - M_2 \tag{3.16}$$

where M_2 indicates the level of imports.

With the help of equation (2.18), (3.16) can be written as:

$$\frac{1}{U_1} \frac{dU}{dp} = (1 - \beta) \frac{dX_2}{dp} - M_2 \tag{3.17}$$

where

$$\beta = \left[\frac{w_1\,dL_1 + r\,dK_1}{\mu w_1\,dL_1 + r\,dK_1} \right] > 0$$

From equation (3.17) all the implications of the changes in the terms of trade for welfare can be derived.

Theorem 3.3: In the first best framework a deterioration (improvement) in the terms of trade lowers (raises) welfare.

   If factor price differentials are absent, then $\beta = 1$, hence the first term in equation (3.18) vanishes. So $(1/U_1)(dU/dp) = -M_2$, which is always negative, indicates a loss in welfare due to a deterioration in the terms of trade. The result is presented geometrically in Figure 3.6. The

Figure 3.6

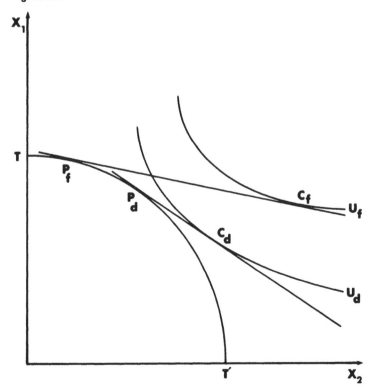

diagram is self-explanatory.

In the presence of a factor price differential $\beta \neq 1$. From (3.17) we know that $\beta \gtrless 1$ as $\mu \lessgtr 1$. Let us suppose that $\mu > 1$ and that there are no value-intensity reversals so that $(dX_2/dp) > 0$. The value of $\mu > 1$ implies $\beta < 1$, $(dX_2/dp) > 0$, so the first term in (3.17) is positive while the second term is negative. It therefore follows that the sign of $(1/U_1)(dU/dp)$ is ambiguous. In other words a deterioration in the terms of trade may raise welfare. Thus, theorem (3.3) does not hold in the presence of a factor price differential.[7]

Theorem 3.4: Theorem 3.3 does not hold in the presence of factor price differentials.

An intuitive explanation of the unexpected result that a deterioration in the terms of trade raises welfare can be obtained by rewriting equation (3.16). By using equations (2.19) to (2.21) equation (3.16) can be written as:

$$\frac{1}{U_1} \frac{dU}{dp} = \frac{dX_1}{d\omega} \frac{d\omega}{dp} + p \frac{dX_2}{d\omega} \frac{d\omega}{dp} - M_2 \qquad (3.18)$$

By using the explicit solutions for $(dX_i/d\omega)$ contained in equations (2.19) and (2.20) and the simplifying assumption that $\sigma_1 = \sigma_2 = \sigma$, (3.18) can be written as:

$$\frac{1}{U_1} \frac{dU}{dp} = \frac{\sigma k(w_1 - w_2)}{(k_2 - k_1)} \frac{d\omega}{dp} - M_2 \qquad (3.19)$$

On the basis of (3.19), we explain the economic mechanism that gives rise to the perverse result already noted. From Chapter 2, we know that:

$$\frac{d\omega}{dp} = \frac{(\mu k_1 - k_2)}{(\omega + k_1)(\mu\omega + k_2)}$$

Given this expression, we can analyse the sign of (3.19). Let us suppose $k_2 > k_1$ and $\mu > 1$. We further assume that value-intensity reversals do not occur, hence, $\mu k_1 - k_2 < 0$. This implies that $(d\omega/dp) < 0$. Now $\mu > 1$ implies that $w_1 < w_2$, so the first term in (3.19) is positive. The second term is negative, hence the ambiguity regarding the sign of $(1/U_1)(dU/dp)$. Now, our only task is the economic explanation of the positive first term. We know that $(d\omega/dp) < 0$ implies that wage–rental ratio falls as a result of an increase in the commodity price ratio. A fall in the wage–rental ratio results in substitution of labour for capital because labour has become the relatively cheaper factor. Hence, both sectors release capital. To maintain full employment of both factors, we know from Rybczynski's theorem that this release in capital must result in an increase in the output of the physically capital-intensive industry, that is X_2. An expansion of X_2 implies that labour is drawn from X_1 into X_2. We also know that $w_2 > w_1$, so labour moves from a low-productivity sector to a high-productivity sector. Therefore, this movement represents a productivity gain for the economy. This is exactly the meaning of the positivity of the first term in (3.19) given our assumptions regarding physical and value intensities and the

Figure 3.7

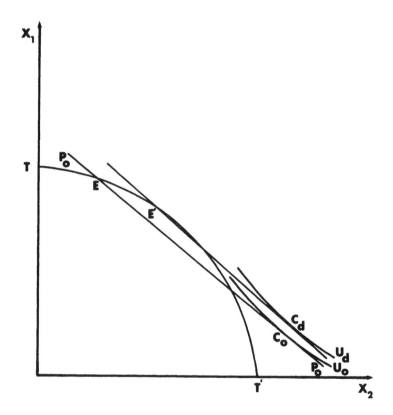

differential. This productivity gain may offset the consumption loss resulting from an adverse movement in the terms of trade giving rise to the possibility that welfare may improve as a consequence of a deterioration in the terms of trade.

This result, that a deterioration in the terms of trade may raise welfare, is presented diagrammatically in Figure 3.7 where TT′ represents the inferior production possibility locus. At the original terms of trade as given by the slope of P_0P_0 production equilibrium occurs at E and consumption equilibrium at C_0. Welfare level is indicated by U_0. Suppose the terms of trade deteriorate, that is p rises. This is indicated by the slope of the line $E'C_d$. Assuming a normal relationship between price and output movements this change in price takes production to E', consumption to C_d and welfare to U_d. It is obvious $U_d > U_0$, so welfare has risen as a consequence of the deterioration in the terms of trade. The diagram clearly shows that the welfare gain occurs due to the wedge that is created by the distortion between the production possibility locus and the commodity price ratio. The non-tangency may not allow the welfare level to decrease as a consequence of the deterioration in the terms of trade, even though the output responds correctly to changes in the price ratio. The wedge, of course, represents the factor price differential.

3.4 Higher versus Lower Tariff

In this section, we consider the proposition that a lower tariff in welfare terms is better than a higher tariff, provided it is assumed that there are no inferior goods in consumption.[8] Let t denote the tariff rate and p_h the domestic price ratio, i.e. $p_h = p(1 + t)$.

By differentiating the utility functions (1.1) and by following the procedure outlined in the section on terms of trade and welfare we arrive at the following expression:

$$\frac{1}{U_1}\frac{dU}{dt} = (1 - \beta)pp_h\frac{dX_2}{dp_h} + tp^2\frac{dM_2}{dp_h} \tag{3.20}$$

On the basis of equation (3.20) several propositions regarding tariffs and welfare can be derived. Only two propositions are presented below.

Theorem 3.5: In the non-distortionary model a higher tariff is welfare-wise worse than a lower tariff, provided inferior goods are ruled out in consumption.

In the first best framework $\beta = 1$, hence (3.20) reduces to:

$$\frac{1}{U_1}\frac{dU}{dt}=tp^2\frac{dM_2}{dp_h}$$

For non-inferior goods $(dM_2/dp_h)<0$, and hence welfare falls as a monotonic function of the rate of tariff. This is a well-known result and is presented in Figure 3.8. TT' in Figure 3.8 is the normal production possibility locus. Let us consider two tariff rates. The equilibrium with the lower tariff rate is indicated by production at P_L and consumption at C_L. The welfare level is indicated by the indifference curve U_L. Now, considering the higher tariff, the production equilibrium moves to P_H and consumption equilibrium to C_H.

Figure 3.8

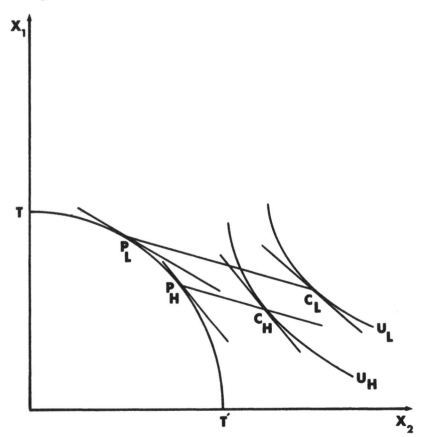

Welfare is indicated by U_H, U_H is lower than U_L, and hence a higher tariff is, welfare-wise, worse than a lower tariff.

In the presence of a single factor price differential the value of $\beta \neq 1$. Hence, the first term in equation (3.20) does not vanish. Let us suppose that $\mu > 1$. This implies that $\beta < 1$ so that $(1 - \beta) > 0$. Let us further assume that $(dX_2/dp_h) > 0$ and $(dM_2/dp_h) < 0$, in other words both these responses are assumed to be normal despite the presence of the differential. This implies that the first term of equation (3.20) is positive, while the second is negative, and therefore the sign of $(1/U_1)(dU/dt)$ is ambiguous. This result again occurs due to the wedge created by the distortion between the inferior production possibility locus and the commodity price ratio. Let us consider the case in which $\mu > 1$, i.e. wages in sector 1 are lower than in sector 2 $(w_1 < w_2)$. This implies that at the point of equilibrium more of X_1 is produced than is socially desirable. A higher tariff (given $(dX_2/dp_h) > 0$) moves production towards the optimal point, and hence reduces the production loss due to the wage differential. The higher tariff no doubt imposes a consumption loss. The total welfare effect depends on these two opposite forces. When production gain exceeds (does not exceed) the consumption loss a higher tariff turns out to be better (worse) than a lower tariff. Thus, in the presence of factor price differentials a higher tariff cannot be ranked uniquely *vis-à-vis* a lower tariff in the welfare sense.

3.5 Summary

In this chapter we have examined the 'gains from trade' theorems, assuming the economy to be characterised by the presence of distortionary factor price differentials. We have arrived at the following results.

(1) In the presence of *a* (single) factor price differential (a) free trade cannot be uniquely ranked *vis-à-vis* no trade; (b) a deterioration (improvement) in the terms of trade does not necessarily lead to deterioration (improvement) in welfare; and (c) a higher tariff cannot be uniquely ranked *vis-à-vis* a lower tariff from the point of view of economic welfare. Result (b) is of some importance for the controversy on the secular deterioration of the terms of trade of less-developed countries. The markets in these countries are known to be highly imperfect.

(2) All the 'gains from trade' theorems hold on the inferior

transformation locus if there are two mutually offsetting factor price differentials.

(3) The optimal policy in the case of *one* factor price differential is a factor tax-cum-subsidy policy. The second best policy is a production tax-cum-subsidy policy.

(4) If there are two factor price differentials then the following cases should be distinguished from the policy point of view.

(a) If the degree of factor price differentials are equal then both the production tax-cum-subsidy policy and the factor tax-cum-subsidy policy lead the economy to a first best solution. Hence, the distinction between first best policy and second best policy emphasised in (3) ceases to exist.

(b) If the factor price differentials are mutually offsetting then a production tax-cum-subsidy policy will not improve welfare. This is so because in this case the economy operates with tangency on the inferior production possibility curve. A factor tax-cum-subsidy policy takes the economy to a first best solution.

Notes

1. 'In other words, if a unanimous decision were required in order for trade to be permitted, it would always be possible for those who desired trade to buy off those opposed to trade, with the result that all could be made better off.' See Samuelson (14), p. 204.

2. The first rigorous proof of this theorem was given by Samuelson (14) in 1939. Theorem 2 is associated with Krueger and Sonnenschein (16) and theorem 3 with Kemp (17).

3. This can be shown quite easily.

$$X_1 + pX_2 = D_1 + pD_2$$

From Chapter 1: $D_1 = X_1 - E_1$

$$D_2 = X_2 + M_2$$

By substitution:

$$\therefore E_1 = pM_2$$

4. This distinction was originally drawn by Johnson (8).

5. It is important to mention that in terms of Bhagwati's (5) definition there is only one distortion in the system even though $r_1 \neq r_2$ and $w_1 \neq w_2$ and they mutually offset each other. This is so because Bhagwati defines four principal types of distortions (three in terms of inequalities in the rates of transformation and the fourth as the shrinkage of the production possibility locus). Thus the number of distortions is determined not in terms of intuitive sources of distortions but in terms of their consequences. We are using the term two, here, in the sense of defining distortions from the source. In this context one should also men-

tion the work of Batra and Pattanaik (1), Magee (20), Herberg, Magee and Kemp (19) and Jones (9), who analyse the consequences of a change in the wage differential μ for other variables of the system. The results obtained belong to both normative and positive economics. As long as the distortions are defined in terms of consequences the results belonging to the former category are not of much interest due to the following statement of Bhagwati (5): 'Reductions in the degree of a distortion will not necessarily be welfare increasing if there is another distortion in the system' (page 86). We call this a statement rather than Proposition 6 because this is not falsifiable – a problem with several other propositions in Bhagwati's otherwise classic and important contribution to trade and distortion theory.

6. This distinction ceases to exist only when one is defining the distortion from the source. However, if the distortion is defined in terms of consequences then there is only one distortion, namely, DRS = FRT ≠ DRT. The optimal policy for this case is of course a production tax-cum-subsidy policy.

7. The breakdown of theorem 3.3 can also occur due to the perverse response of output to a price change. A detailed analysis of this particular result has been omitted.

8. The restriction that inferior goods should be ruled out for this proposition was first pointed out by Bhagwati (2).

References

Free Trade versus No Trade With and Without Factor Price Differentials and Optimal Policy

(1) Batra, R. N., and Pattanaik, P. K. 1971. Factor Market Imperfections: The Terms of Trade and Welfare. *American Economic Review*, Vol. 61 (December), 946–55.

(2) Bhagwati, J. N., and Ramaswami, V. K. 1963. Domestic Distortions, Tariffs and the Theory of Optimum Subsidy. *Journal of Political Economy*, Vol. 71 (February), 44–50.

(3) Bhagwati, J. N. 1968. The Gains from Trade Once Again. *Oxford Economic Papers*, Vol. 20 (July), 137–48.

(4) Bhagwati, J. N., Ramaswami, V. K., and Srinivasan, T. N. 1969. Domestic Distortions, Tariffs and the Theory of Optimum Subsidy: Some Further Results. *Journal of Political Economy*, Vol. 77 (September), 1005–10.

(5) Bhagwati, J. N. 1971. The Generalized Theory of Distortions and Welfare. In J. N. Bhagwati, R. W. Jones, R. Mundell and J. Vanek (eds.), *Trade, Balance of Payments and Growth*. Papers in International Economics in Honour of Charles P. Kindleberger. Amsterdam: North Holland.

(6) Hazari, B. R. 1974. Factor Market Distortions and Gains from Trade Revisited. *Weltwirtschaftliches Archiv*, Vol. 110 (October), 413–29.

(7) Hazari, B. R., and Pattanaik, P. K. 1977. Some Welfare Propositions in a Three Commodity Three Factor Model of Trade. Mimeographed (May).

(8) Johnson, H. G. 1965. Optimal Trade Intervention in the Presence of Domestic Distortions. In R. E. Caves, H. G. Johnson and P. B. Kenen (eds.), *Money, Trade and Growth: Essays in Honour of G. Haberler*. Chicago: Rand-McNally.

(9) Jones, R. W. 1971. Distortions in Factor Markets and the General Equilibrium Model of Production. *Journal of Political Economy*, Vol. 79 (May/June), 437–59.

(10) Kemp, M. C. 1962. The Gain from International Trade. *Economic Journal*, Vol. 72 (December), 803–19.

(11) Kemp, M. C., and Negishi, T. 1969. Domestic Distortions, Tariffs and the Theory of Optimum Subsidy. *Journal of Political Economy*, Vol. 77 (November), 1011–13.

(12) Ricardo, D. 1817. *On the Principles of Political Economy and Taxation.* London: John Murray.

(13) Samuelson, P. A. 1939. The Gains from International Trade. *Canadian Journal of Economics and Political Science*, Vol. 5 (May), 195–205.

(14) Samuelson, P. A. 1962. The Gains from International Trade Once Again. *Economic Journal*, Vol. 62 (December), 820–9.

On Terms of Trade and Welfare

(15) Batra, R. N., and Pattanaik, P. K. 1970. Domestic Distortions and the Gains from Trade. *Economic Journal*, Vol. 80 (September), 638–49.

(16) Krueger, A. O., and Sonnenschein, H. 1967. The Terms of Trade, the Gains from Trade and Price Divergence. *International Economic Review*, Vol. 8 (February), 121–7.

See also Hazari (6).

On Tariffs and Welfare

(17) Kemp, M. C. 1969. *The Pure Theory of International Trade and Investment*, Ch. 12. Englewood Cliffs, New Jersey: Prentice-Hall.

(18) Ohyama, M. 1972. Domestic Distortions and the Theory of Tariffs. *Keio Economic Studies*, Vol. 1, 1–14.

See also Hazari (6).

On Variations in the Degree of Distortions

(19) Herberg, H., Kemp, M. C., and Magee, S. P. 1971. Factor Market Distortions, the Reversal of Relative Factor Intensities and the Relation Between Product Prices and Equilibrium Outputs. *Economic Record*, Vol. 47 (December), 518–30.

(20) Magee, S. P. 1971. Factor Market Distortions, Production and the Pure Theory of International Trade. *Quarterly Journal of Economics*, Vol. 85 (November), 623–43.

See also (1), (5), (6) and (9).

4 FACTOR PRICE DIFFERENTIALS, ECONOMIC EXPANSION AND WELFARE

In this chapter we explore the implications of economic expansion for output levels, real factor rewards and welfare for a single small country, on the assumption that the economy is characterised by a factor price differential. The differential is assumed to exist in the labour market while the capital market is assumed to be non-distorted. Economic expansion can occur from various sources. Within the framework of our model, the two obvious sources of expansion are (a) technical progress (biased or unbiased) and (b) factor accumulation. The implications of technical progress are considered first.

4.1 Technical Progress

The concept of technical progress is generally introduced via the production function. In its most general form the production function incorporating technical progress can be written as:

$$X_i = F_i(K_i, L_i, t) \quad i = 1, 2 \tag{4.1}$$

where t denotes the state of technology. For any given conditions of technology the function F_i in (4.1) is assumed to possess the properties as outlined for production functions in Chapter 1. It is also assumed that $(\partial F_i/\partial t) > 0$.

On the basis of equation (4.1) various types of technical progress can be defined. Our analysis will be confined to Hicks-neutral technical progress[1]. This is defined as an increase in the marginal product of both inputs in the same proportion at the original equilibrium factor price ratio.[2] Biased technical progress can be defined quite easily from the above definition of neutrality. For instance, if at the original factor price ratio, technical progress raises the marginal product of capital more than that of labour, then technical progress is defined as capital-using or labour-saving.

In the case of Hicks-neutral technical progress (4.1) can be written in the following more explicit form:

$$X_i = \lambda_i F_i(K_i, L_i) \quad i = 1, 2 \tag{4.2}$$

where λ_i indicates technical progress. We shall assume that technical progress only occurs in the first industry so that:

$$X_1 = \lambda_1 F_1(K_1, L_1) = \lambda_1 L_1 f_1(k_1) \tag{4.3}$$

$$X_2 = F_2(K_2, L_2) = L_2 f_2(k_2) \tag{4.4}$$

The introduction of technical progress in industry 1 obviously affects the marginal productivity conditions. Given our assumptions that $\mu w_1 = w_2$ and $r_1 = r_2 = r$, the new marginal conditions are:

$$r = \lambda_1 f_1' = pf_2' \tag{4.5}$$

$$\mu w_1 = w_2 = \lambda_1 \mu (f_1 - k_1 f_1') = p(f_2 - k_2 f_2') \tag{4.6}$$

The rest of the equations of the model presented in Chapter 1 remain unchanged.

4.2 Technical Progress, Factor Intensities, Factor Prices and Output Levels

This section analyses the consequences of Hicks-neutral technical progress for factor intensities, factor prices and output levels. We first obtain expressions for factor intensities. By differentiating equations (4.5) and (4.6) with respect to λ_1, holding commodity prices constant, we obtain the following solution for the response of factor intensities:

$$\frac{dk_1}{d\lambda_1} = \frac{pf_2}{\lambda_1^2 f_1''(\mu k_1 - k_2)} \tag{4.7}$$

$$\frac{dk_2}{d\lambda_1} = \frac{f_1}{pf_2''(\mu k_1 - k_2)} \tag{4.8}$$

In the non-distortionary case ($\mu = 1$), the direction of change in the variables k_1, k_2 depends on $k_1 \gtrless k_2$, that is the difference between the physical-factor intensities of the two industries. However, in the presence of a factor price differential the sign depends on value-factor intensities, i.e. $\mu k_1 \gtrless k_2$.[3] The signs of $dk_1/d\lambda_1$ and $dk_2/d\lambda_1$ can be determined from equations (4.7) and (4.8).

Suppose the first industry is capital-intensive in the physical and value sense, that is, $k_1 > k_2$ and $\mu k_1 > k_2$. These physical and value intensities can prevail for $\mu > 1$, or $\mu < 1$ but not sufficiently small to cause a value-intensity reversal. If $k_1 > k_2$ and $\mu k_1 > k_2$, then it follows from (4.7) and (4.8) that capital intensities fall in both sectors as a result of neutral technical progress in sector 1. In other words, as a consequence of technical progress labour is substituted for capital in both sectors. The intuitive explanation of this result runs along the following lines. Technical progress in sector 1 lowers the cost of production of commodity 1, hence raising the original relative price of commodity 2. However, given our assumption of fixed commodity price ratio the original price ratio must be maintained. This original price ratio can only be maintained by a change in the factor price ratio such that the relative price of commodity 2 falls to the original level. In other words, the price of factors employed in sector 1 must rise so that the price of good 1 rises to establish the original commodity price ratio. This can happen via an increase in the price of the factor used intensively in sector 1, i.e. rental on capital rises relative to the wage rate. Since the rental on capital rises relative to the wage rate, labour must be substituted for capital, which implies that both k_1 and k_2 must fall. This is exactly what we have obtained. The formal expressions for change in the real reward of factors are given below:

$$\frac{dr}{d\lambda_1} = \frac{f_1}{(\mu k_1 - k_2)} \tag{4.9}$$

$$\frac{dw_2}{d\lambda_1} = -\frac{k_2 f_1}{(\mu k_1 - k_2)} \tag{4.10}$$

Equations (4.9) and (4.10) confirm what has already been said about the movement in rental on capital and wage rate.

Let us suppose instead that value intensities reverse, so that $k_1 > k_2$ but $\mu k_1 < k_2$. Such a reversal can occur when $\mu < 1$ ($w_1 > w_2$), in other words not only the physically capital-intensive sector pays the premium to labour but is such that the physically capital-intensive sector becomes labour-intensive in a value sense. The reversal of value intensities leads to a change in the sign of $dk_i/d\lambda_1$. Given $k_1 > k_2$ and $\mu k_1 < k_2$, it follows from (4.7) and (4.8) that technical progress results in an increase in capital intensity in both the sectors. This sign is opposite to the one obtained in the non-distortionary framework and in the non-value-intensity reversal case. The intuitive explanation of this result runs parallel to the one given for the standard result. As in the previous case, technical progress in sector 1 lowers the cost of production of commodity 1, hence raising the original relative price of commodity 2. However, given our assumption that the country is small the original commodity price ratio must be maintained. This can only happen by a change in the factor price ratio. The original price ratio can be maintained through a rise in the price of factors employed intensively in the value sense by sector 1. Sector 1 is labour-intensive in a value sense, and hence technical progress results in an increase in the wage rate relative to the rental on capital. (Refer to equations (4.9) and (4.10).) This change in factor prices naturally results in the substitution of capital for labour, i.e. an increase in the capital intensities as a result of technical progress in sector 1. Notice, here, the important role played by the divorce between the physical ranking of sectors and the value ranking of sectors. The value ranking of sectors governs the price changes, hence the non-normal response of wage–rental ratio giving rise to the non-normal response of capital intensities. In the standard case the two rankings are identical, so the non-normal response cannot occur.

We are now equipped to analyse the impact of technical progress in sector 1 on the output levels of commodities 1 and 2. By differentiating equations (4.3) and (4.4):

$$\frac{dX_1}{d\lambda_1} = \lambda_1 L_1 f_1' \frac{dk_1}{d\lambda_1} + \lambda_1 f_1 \frac{dL_1}{d\lambda_1} + L_1 f_1 \tag{4.11}$$

$$\frac{dX_2}{d\lambda_1} = L_2 f_2' \frac{dk_2}{d\lambda_1} + f_2 \frac{dL_2}{d\lambda_1} \tag{4.12}$$

Explicit solutions for $dL_1/d\lambda_1$ and $dL_2/d\lambda_1$ can be obtained from the factor endowment conditions. By substituting these solutions in (4.11) and (4.12) and simplifying, we obtain:

$$\frac{dX_1}{d\lambda_1} = L_1 f_1 - L_1 \frac{(rk_2 + w_2)}{(k_1 - k_2)} \frac{dk_1}{d\lambda_1} - \frac{\lambda_1 f_1 L_2}{(k_1 - k_2)} \frac{dk_2}{d\lambda_1} \tag{4.13}$$

$$\frac{dX_2}{d\lambda_1} = \frac{L_2(\mu w_1 + rk_1)}{(k_1 - k_2)} \frac{dk_2}{d\lambda_1} + \frac{L_1 f_2}{(k_1 - k_2)} \frac{dk_1}{d\lambda_1} \tag{4.14}$$

On the basis of equations (4.13) and (4.14) the output responses can be determined. Two cases are considered: (a) the standard result that neutral technical progress results in an increase (decrease) in the output of the industry in which neutral technical progress occurs (does not occur); and (b) the non-standard result, due to the presence of a factor price differential, that neutral technical progress may result in an increase (decrease) in the output of the industry in which technical progress does not occur (occurs).

Let us suppose that $k_1 > k_2$ and $\mu \gtrless 1$ but such that $\mu k_1 > k_2$. From equations (4.7) and (4.8), we know that $dk_1/d\lambda_1$ and $dk_2/d\lambda_1$ are negative. If both $dk_i/d\lambda_1$ (i = 1, 2) are negative, then it follows from (4.13) that all the expressions on the right-hand side of the equation are positive, hence output of X_1 increases. The sign of X_2 depends on the sign of $dk_i/d\lambda_1$ (i = 1, 2). Since these are negative for $k_1 > k_2$, output of X_2 falls as a result of neutral technical progress in sector 1. The economic explanation of this result follows. Neutral technical progress in sector 1, given our assumptions that $k_1 > k_2$ and $\mu k_1 > k_2$, results in an increase in the rental on capital and a decrease in the wage rate. This causes substitution of labour for capital (a decrease in the k_i's). From the factor endowment conditions to preserve full employment a fall in k_i's implies that L_1 must rise and L_2 fall. Since both k_2 and L_2 fall, output of X_2 falls, and of course output of X_1 rises.

Let us now suppose that $k_1 > k_2$ but $\mu k_1 < k_2$ ($\mu < 1$). This implies that the physically capital-intensive sector pays a premium to labour. Moreover, the physical ranking of the sectors is no longer the same as the value ranking. With $k_1 > k_2$ and $\mu k_1 < k_2$ the signs of the response of capital-labour ratios change from the normal case. From (4.7) and (4.8) we know that in the case of value-intensity reversal $dk_1/d\lambda_1$ and $dk_2/d\lambda_1$ are positive (because $\mu k_1 - k_2 < 0$, f_i'''s < 0). From (4.14) if both the capital-labour ratios rise the output of X_2 must rise. In other words, the output of the non-progressive sector rises. However, the output response of sector 1 is ambiguous. In equation (4.13) the first term is always positive, but due to value-intensity reversal the sign of the other two terms is negative, hence the ambiguity of the sign of the output response in sector 1.[4] The economic explanation of the result is obtained from examining the movement in the wage–rental ratio. Value-intensity reversals lead to an increase in the wage rate and a fall in the rental on capital. Hence the wage–rental ratio rises. The increase in the wage–rental ratio causes substitution of capital for labour, and labour therefore becomes the factor in excess supply. This implies that the physically labour-intensive sector must expand, which happens to be X_2, the non-progressive sector, in our case.

These results can be represented geometrically. In Figures 4.1 and 4.2 the standard and non-standard results in the presence of distortions are presented. Since a verbal explanation of the standard result has already been given, we shall only offer a detailed explanation of Figure 4.2, which presents the non-standard result.

In Figure 4.2 the producers of commodity 2 face the factor price ratio given by the slope of the line AB while the producers of commodity 1 face the factor price ratio given by the slope of line AC. The slope of the line AC is greater than that of AB, indicating that sector 1 pays the premium to labour. The tangency of production isoquants with the wage–rental ratio indicates a point of equilibrium. The initial equilibrium is assumed to occur at point R_2 for sector 2 and at point R_1 for sector 1. The slope of OR_1 is greater than that of OR_2, indicating that sector 1 is physically capital-intensive relative to sector 2 ($k_1 > k_2$). The total endowment is given by point E which

Figure 4.1

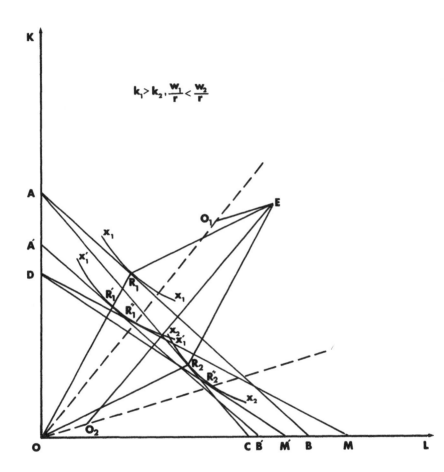

Figure 4.2

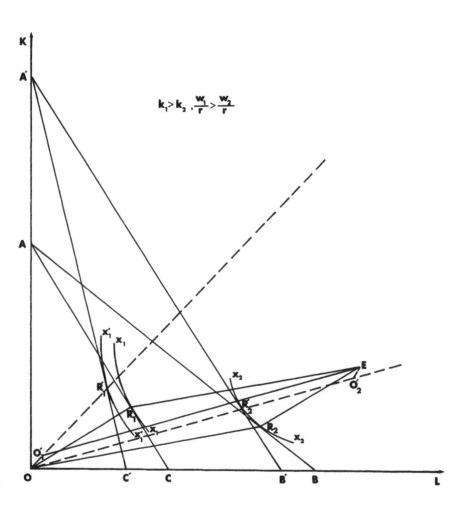

equals the sum of vectors OR_1 and OR_2, indicating that both the factors
are fully employed. Let us now suppose that neutral technical progress
takes place in sector 1. This shifts the isoquant of sector 1 to $x_1'x_1'$
indicating a lowering of costs. Note that at constant wage—rental ratio
the capital intensity of sector 1 is unaltered, indicating that the technical progress satisfies the definition of Hicks neutrality. Assuming value-
intensity reversal, we know from equations (4.7) and (4.8) that the new
equilibrium position occurs at a point at which the capital intensities in
both sectors have increased ($k_1 > k_2$, $\mu k_1 < k_2$). From equations (4.9)
and (4.10) we also know that the wage—rental ratio increases. The
differential is assumed to remain constant. Let the new wage—rental
ratio in sector 1 be indicated by the slope of the line $A'C'$ and in sector
2 by the line $A'B'$. The new factor intensities are indicated by OR_1' and
OR_2'. We now have to work out the output response. Since the system
is assumed to maintain full employment output levels can be obtained
by drawing from E, lines parallel to the new factor-intensity rays
(dashed lines), giving EO_1' (parallel to OR_2') and EO_2' (parallel to OR_1').
These indicate output levels OO_1' and OO_2', which show that the output
of progressive industry falls and that of non-progressive industry rises as
a result of technical progress.

We can summarise our results in terms of the following theorems
(assuming that the country is small):

Theorem 4.1: If $\mu \lessgtr 1$, $k_1 > k_2$ and $\mu k_1 > k_2$ then Hicks-neutral technical progress in sector 1 results in a decline in the factor intensities
(k_1, k_2) in both sectors, an increase in the rental on capital, a fall in the
wage rate and an increase (decrease) in the output of sector 1 (sector
2).[5]

Theorem 4.2: If the capital-intensive sector pays the premium to
labour ($\mu < 1$, $k_1 > k_2$) and value-intensity reversal occurs ($\mu k_1 < k_2$)
then neutral technical progress in sector 1 results in a rise in the factor
intensities (k_1, k_2) in both sectors, a decline in the rental on capital, an
increase in the wage rate and an increase in the output of the non-
progressive sector 2 (X_2).

Theorem 4.3: A necessary condition for the perverse response of output
to neutral technical progress is value-intensity reversal.

4.3 Factor Accumulation and Output Levels

In the last section, we obtained the interesting result that technical progress in the presence of a wage differential may lead to a perverse output response. However, in the case of factor accumulation output responses are the same as in the first best framework, and perverse output responses do not occur. This is because factor accumulation takes place at constant commodity and factor prices, in contrast with technical progress which occurs at constant commodity but non-constant factor prices. At constant factor and commodity prices value-intensity reversals cannot occur, hence factor accumulation results in output movements that behave according to the Rybczynski theorem. The case of capital accumulation is presented geometrically in Figure 4.3, in which the output of the capital-intensive good necessarily rises in spite of the presence of a wage differential. In a similar manner the

Figure 4.3

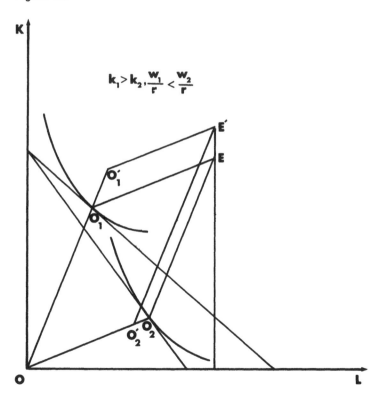

case of growth in the labour supply can be analysed.

4.4 Economic Expansion and Welfare

This section is devoted to an analysis of the impact of economic expansion on welfare. We shall first discuss the consequences of technical progress on welfare and then proceed to discuss the impact of capital and labour accumulation on welfare. In the final section we shall discuss the difference between a welfare change due to technical progress and that due to factor accumulation.

By differentiating the utility function (1.1) with respect to λ_1 (holding prices constant) and suitable arrangement of terms we obtain:

$$\frac{1}{U_1} \frac{dU}{d\lambda_1} = \frac{dD_1}{d\lambda_1} + p \frac{dD_2}{d\lambda_1} \tag{4.15}$$

Equation (4.15) can be rewritten in the following form, by differentiating equations (1.3), (1.4) and (1.5) with respect to λ_1 (holding prices constant) and substitution in (4.15):

$$\frac{1}{U_1} \frac{dU}{d\lambda_1} = \frac{dX_1}{d\lambda_1} + p \frac{dX_2}{d\lambda_1} \tag{4.16}$$

Expression (4.16) can be simplified by obtaining an expression for the slope of the new production possibility curve in terms of the pre-technical progress production possibility locus. This is given below:

$$\frac{dX_1}{dX_2} = -pz \quad \text{where} \quad z = \frac{w_1 dL_1 + rdK_1 + F_1 d\lambda_1}{\mu w_1 dL_1 + rdK_1} > 0 \tag{4.17}$$

$F_1 d\lambda_1$ indicates the shift factor, which appears due to technical progress[6] and is always positive. It is obvious from (4.17) that $z \lessgtr 1$ as $\mu > 1$ and $z > 1$ whenever $\mu < 1$.

By utilising equation (4.17), (4.16) can be written as:

$$\frac{1}{U_1} \frac{dU}{d\lambda_1} = \left(\frac{z-1}{z} \right) \frac{dX_1}{d\lambda_1} \tag{4.18}$$

Equation (4.18) provides us with the expression that indicates the change in welfare as a consequence of technical progress in sector 1. We now present several interesting results regarding normal and 'immiserising growth'.

It is obvious from (4.18) that normal growth only occurs if both the terms on the right-hand side are of the same sign. 'Immiserising growth' occurs when the two terms are of opposite signs, i.e. $(z - 1)/z \gtrless 0$

and $(dX_1/d\lambda_1) \lesseqgtr 0$. A detailed treatment of these cases follows.

Let us suppose that $k_1 > k_2$. We suppose further that $\mu > 1$ which implies that value-intensity reversals cannot occur, and hence neutral technical progress results in an increase in the output of sector 1, so that $(dX_1/d\lambda_1) > 0$. However, when $\mu > 1$, $z \lessgtr 1$. The sign of the first term in (4.18) depends on z, $(z - 1)/z \gtreqless 0$ as $z \gtreqless 1$. Thus, if $z > 1$, then welfare increases as a result of technical progress and if $z < 1$ then welfare falls as a result of technical progress. The latter phenomenon is known as 'immiserising growth'.

In Figures 4.4a and 4.4b we present both the above-mentioned results geometrically. In the process of explaining the diagram, we also offer an intuitive explanation of the result on 'immiserising growth'. In Figure 4.4a TT and TT' represent the pre-growth and post-growth production possibility locus. The pre-growth production equilibrium occurs at P_0, consumption equilibrium at C_0 and welfare level is indicated by U_0. Technical progress results in an outward movement of the production possibility locus which is given by TT'. On this new locus production equilibrium occurs at P_g, consumption equilibrium at C_g, and the welfare level is indicated by U_g. Since $U_g > U_0$, welfare increases as a result of technical progress in sector 1.

In Figure 4.4b, the case of 'immiserising growth' is presented. The pre-growth production possibility locus is given by TT and the post-growth production possibility locus is given by TT'. The pre-growth production equilibrium is given by $\hat{P}_0$, consumption equilibrium by $\hat{C}_0$ and the welfare level by U'_0. The post-growth production equilibrium is indicated by P''_g, consumption equilibrium by C''_g and welfare by U''_g. It is obvious that $U''_g < U'_0$; hence welfare decreases as a consequence of technical progress.

The intuitive explanation of this result can be derived by examining the direction of μ. We have assumed that $\mu > 1$ and $k_1 > k_2$. In this case value-intensity reversals cannot occur, hence $(dX_1/d\lambda_1) > 0$, so that the output of the progressive industry increases. The value of $\mu > 1$ implies that $w_1 < w_2$. Since $(dX_1/d\lambda_1) > 0$ it pulls labour away from a high-productivity sector to a low-productivity sector. This movement of labour causes a social loss. If this loss is greater than the productivity gain due to technical progress then 'immiserising growth' occurs, which is precisely the case in Figure 4.4b. The important thing to note is that 'immiserising growth' occurs without value-intensity reversal and is caused due to the wedge term which indicates the direction of the wage differential.

Let us suppose now that $k_1 > k_2$ and $\mu < 1$, such that $\mu k_1 < k_2$. In

Figure 4.4a

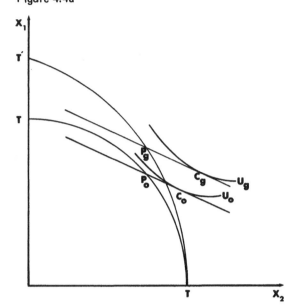

Figure 4.4b

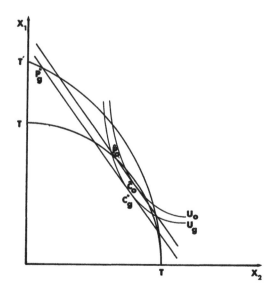

other words, sector 1 is physically capital-intensive but labour-intensive in value sense. When $\mu < 1$, we know from equation (4.17) that $z > 1$. Hence $(z - 1)/z > 0$. Let us suppose that due to value-intensity reversals the output of sector 1 responds perversely to technical progress, i.e. $(dX_1/d\lambda_1) < 0$. Since $(z - 1)/z > 0$ and $(dX_1/d\lambda_1) < 0$ it follows from (4.18) that $(1/U_1)(dU/d\lambda_1) < 0$. Thus 'immiserising growth' occurs due to a perverse movement of output to technical progress. This result is presented geometrically in Figure 4.5. In Figure 4.5, P_0 is the point of production equilibrium in the pre-growth situation and P_g is the point of production equilibrium in the post-growth situation. Note that the output of sector 1 has decreased due to technical progress in sector 1. Post-growth welfare is indicated by U_g and pre-growth welfare level by U_0. Since, $U_g < U_0$, technical progress results in a decline in welfare.

Figure 4.5

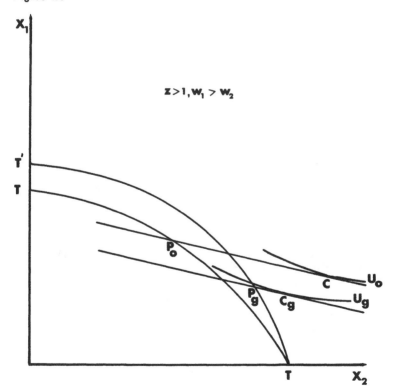

The explanation of this result is quite simple. Since $\mu < 1$, we know that $w_1 > w_2$. Output of X_1 falls, so that labour moves again from the high-productivity sector to the low-productivity sector, resulting in 'immiserising growth'. This result is caused by perverse response of output due to value-intensity reversal.[7]

We now proceed to derive results relating to the impact of factor accumulation on welfare. By differentiating the utility function (1.1) with respect to labour and capital and by following the procedure outlined earlier, we obtain:

$$\frac{1}{U_1}\frac{dU}{dK} = \frac{dX_1}{dK} + p\frac{dX_2}{dK} \tag{4.19}$$

$$\frac{1}{U_1}\frac{dU}{dL} = \frac{dX_1}{dL} + p\frac{dX_2}{dL} \tag{4.20}$$

By using equations (1.19) and (1.20) and substitution in (4.19); and by using equations (1.21) and (1.22) and substitution in (4.20), we obtain:

$$\frac{1}{U_1}\frac{dU}{dK} = \frac{(\mu - 1)w_1}{(k_2 - k_1)} + r \tag{4.21}$$

$$\frac{1}{U_1}\frac{dU}{dL} = \frac{w_1(\mu k_1 - k_2)}{(k_1 - k_2)} \tag{4.22}$$

or

$$\frac{1}{U_1}\frac{dU}{dL} = \frac{(\mu - 1)k_1 w_1}{(k_1 - k_2)} + w_1$$

It is obvious from (4.21) and (4.22) that 'immiserising growth' may arise due to capital and labour accumulation in the presence of a factor price differential. The reason for the occurrence of 'immiserising growth' due to factor accumulation is the wedge term indicating the direction of the differential. For instance, in the case of capital accumulation 'immiserising growth' arises when $\mu < 1$, $k_2 > k_1$, and $[(\mu - 1)w_1/(k_2 - k_1)] + r < 0$. This happens because when $k_2 > k_1$, sector 2 expands as a result of capital accumulation. Since $\mu < 1$ implies $w_1 > w_2$, labour moves from a high-productivity sector to a low-productivity sector. The economy suffers a loss in productivity which is measured by $[(\mu - 1)w_1/(k_2 - k_1)]$. The gain from capital accumulation is indicated by r. If the gain is less than the loss, 'immiserising growth' occurs. A similar interpretation can be provided for equation (4.22).

4.5 Summary

A summary of results on economic expansion and welfare is presented below:

(1) In the presence of a wage differential, Hicks-neutral technical progress may result in a fall (increase) in the output of the sector in which technical progress occurs (does not occur). This result is caused by value-intensity reversal. However, factor accumulation results in a normal output response despite the presence of a differential.

(2) Economic expansion (technical progress or factor accumulation) in the presence of a differential may result in 'immiserising growth'.

(3) When technical progress results in 'immiserising growth', it is due to reallocation of labour from a high-productivity sector to a low-productivity sector. This can happen when the progressive sector expands but pays a lower wage or when the non-progressive sector expands but pays a lower wage. The latter result is of course related with 'value'-intensity reversal which may cause the growth of the non-progressive sector of the economy.

(4) Factor accumulation always results in normal response of output levels. Hence, in this case 'immiserising growth' cannot be caused by the perverse response of output to factor accumulation. 'Immiserising growth' occurs due to the reallocation of labour from a high- to a low-productivity sector. In the factor accumulation case such a reallocation always occurs via the normal response of the output level to factor accumulation.

Notes

1. The consequences of biased technical progress for output levels, real factor rewards and welfare are discussed in Hazari (4).

2. Hicks-neutral technical progress can be easily shown in terms of the isoquant diagram. Suppose in the figure below that the original equilibrium occurs at points e_1 and e_2 where the output $X_1 = 1$ and $X_2 = 1$. Now suppose that technical progress occurs in sector 1. This shifts the $x_1 x_1$ isoquant to $x_1' x_1'$. One unit of x_1 is now produced by any point on the $x_1' x_1'$ isoquant. If this shift is such that at the original factor price ratio the marginal products of capital and labour increase in the same proportion, then technical progress is Hicks-neutral. This in fact is the case in the diagram because the slope at e' is the same as at e_1. A more detailed discussion is available in Hicks (1).

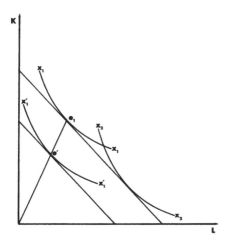

3. A detailed treatment of the distinction between physical intensities and value intensities has already been provided in Chapter 2.

4. Bhagwati (2) in his famous paper on 'immiserising growth' assumes that the output of the industry experiencing technical progress increases in the presence of factor price differentials. This is not necessarily the case in the presence of a wage differential as shown by equation (4.13).

5. This result is the same as obtained by Findlay and Grubert (3).

6. The presence of $F_1 d\lambda_1$ in (4.17) does not imply that in the standard model there will be non-tangency between the production possibility locus and the price line. This term appears because the slope of the new locus is being expressed in terms of the old locus. The correctness of the expression can be easily verified. Moreover, we show below that when $\mu = 1$, $(1/U_1)(dU/d\lambda_1) = F_1 > 0$ which is the normal expression for change in welfare as a consequence of technical progress. Suppose $\mu = 1$. This implies that

$$z = 1 + \frac{F_1 d\lambda_1}{wdL_1 + rdK_1} = 1 + \frac{F_1 d\lambda_1}{dX_1 - F_1 d\lambda_1}$$

Hence, $-(dX_1/pz) = dX_2$. By substituting for dX_2 in equation (4.16), we obtain:

$$\frac{1}{U_1} \frac{dU}{d\lambda_1} = \frac{dX_1}{d\lambda_1} - p\left[\frac{1}{pz} \frac{dX_1}{d\lambda_1} \right]$$

$$= \frac{dX_1}{d\lambda_1} - \left[\frac{dX_1 - F_1 d\lambda_1}{dX_1} \right] \frac{dX_1}{d\lambda_1}$$

$$= \frac{dX_1}{d\lambda_1} - \frac{dX_1}{d\lambda_1} + F_1$$

$$= F_1 > 0$$

7. Bhagwati (2) in his well known paper on 'immiserising growth' does not discuss the case of perverse response of output to technical progress as a cause of 'immiserising growth'.

References

On the Definition of Technical Change

(1) Hicks, J. R. 1932. *The Theory of Wages*. London: Macmillan.

On Technical Change, Factor Intensities, Factor Rewards, Output Levels and Welfare (With and Without Differentials)

(2) Bhagwati, J. N. 1968. Distortions and Immiserizing Growth: A Generalization. *Review of Economic Studies*, Vol. 35 (October), 481–5.

(3) Findlay, R., and Grubert, H. 1959. Factor Intensity, Technological Progress and the Terms of Trade. *Oxford Economic Papers*, new series, Vol. II (February), 111–21.

(4) Hazari, B. R. 1975. Factor Market Distortions, Technical Progress and Trade. *Oxford Economic Papers*, new series, Vol. 27 (March), 47–60.

5 FACTOR PRICE DIFFERENTIALS, ECONOMIC EXPANSION, TERMS OF TRADE AND WELFARE AT VARIABLE TERMS OF TRADE

Interest in the impact of economic expansion on terms of trade dates back to Edgeworth, who conjectured that the expanding country might be worse off after expansion than before. This possibility was shown to be true in an important contribution by Bhagwati (2). Interest in the above-mentioned problem has also been rekindled in recent years by the dollar problem and the Prebisch (14) hypothesis regarding the secular deterioration in the terms of trade of developing nations. In Chapter 4, we analysed the implications of economic expansion for output levels, real factor rewards and welfare in the distortionary framework, given the assumption that the terms of trade are held constant. The analysis of the above-mentioned issues provides us with the necessary ingredients for examining the impact of economic expansion on terms of trade and welfare at variable terms of trade. The factor price differential is assumed to exist in the labour market while the market for capital is assumed to be non-distorted. We shall first consider the implications of technical progress and factor accumulation (the two sources of growth) on terms of trade.

5.1 Technical Progress and Terms of Trade

Here we examine the impact of technical progress on terms of trade, using comparative statics to arrive at an expression that indicates the impact of technical progress on terms of trade.[1] The technique adopted is to evaluate the change in the home demand for imports arising from technical progress at constant terms of trade, i.e. at the original terms of trade. This indicates the direction of the shift in the offer curve of the home country. Obviously the terms of trade of the expanding country deteriorate, improve or remain unchanged depending on whether the demand for imports rises, falls or remains unchanged as a consequence of technical progress.

We now seek a formal expression indicating the impact of technical progress on terms of trade. It is assumed that the foreign country is stationary; in other words technical progress only occurs in the home country. Obviously, technical progress in the home country affects the home demand for imports, and therefore leads to a modification of the balance of payments condition. The balance of payments condition in the presence of technical progress assumes the following form:

$$E_1(p) - pM_2(p, \lambda_1) = 0 \tag{5.1}$$

In equation (5.1) the demand for imports M_2 is a function of relative prices and the agent responsible for economic expansion, λ_1, which indicates the occurrence of Hicks-neutral technical progress in sector 1, the exporting sector of the economy.[2] By differentiating equation (5.1) totally with respect to λ_1 and using the equilibrium condition that $M_2 = (E_1/p)$, we obtain:

$$p\frac{\partial M_2}{\partial \lambda_1} = \left[\frac{p}{E_1} \frac{\partial E_1}{\partial p} - \frac{p}{M_2} \frac{\partial M_2}{\partial p} - 1 \right] M_2 \frac{dp}{d\lambda_1}$$

$$= [\epsilon_f + \epsilon_h - 1] M_2 \frac{dp}{d\lambda_1} \tag{5.2}$$

where $\epsilon_f = (p/E_1)(\partial E_1/\partial p)$ is the elasticity for demand for exports (or foreigners' demand for imports), $\epsilon_h = -(p/M_2)(\partial M_2/\partial p)$ is the elasticity for demand for imports. Let us choose commodity units such that $p = 1$ initially. Now (5.2) can be written as:

$$\frac{dp}{d\lambda_1} = \frac{\dfrac{\partial M_2}{\partial \lambda_1}}{[\epsilon_f + \epsilon_h - 1] M_2} \tag{5.3}$$

which indicates the impact of technical progress on terms of trade. The Marshall–Lerner stability conditions require that $\epsilon_f + \epsilon_h - 1 > 0$. It is well known that in the presence of a wage differential the stability conditions may not be satisfied.[3] We shall, however, assume that the Marshall–Lerner stability conditions are always satisfied. If this stability assumption is not adopted then there is not much point in analysing the comparative static properties of the model. Given this stability assumption, the sign of $dp/d\lambda_1$ depends on the sign of $\partial M_2/\partial \lambda_1$, because $M_2 > 0$. In other words, the change in the terms of trade as a consequence of technical progress depends on the change in imports, $(dp/d\lambda_1) \gtrless 0$ according to $(\partial M_2/\partial \lambda_1) \gtrless 0$. The terms of trade deteriorate (remain constant) or improve depending on an increase (no change) or a decrease in the level of imports. A more explicit expression for the change in the terms of trade can be derived by utilising equation (1.4) which can be written as:

$$M_2 = D_2(p, Y) - X_2(p, \lambda_1) \tag{5.4}$$

where Y indicates national income in terms of commodity 1, i.e.

$Y = X_1 + pX_2$. Differentiate (5.4) with respect to λ_1, holding prices constant to obtain:

$$\frac{\partial M_2}{\partial \lambda_1} = \frac{\partial D_2}{\partial Y}\frac{\partial Y}{\partial \lambda_1} - \frac{\partial X_2}{\partial \lambda_1} = m_h \frac{\partial Y}{\partial \lambda_1} - \frac{\partial X_2}{\partial \lambda_1} \tag{5.5}$$

where $m_h = p(\partial D_2/\partial Y) = (\partial D_2/\partial Y)$ is the marginal propensity to consume importables in the home country. The change in income at constant prices is given by:

$$\frac{\partial Y}{\partial \lambda_1} = \frac{\partial X_1}{\partial \lambda_1} + p\frac{\partial X_2}{\partial \lambda_1} \tag{5.6}$$

Equation (5.6) can be simplified by using equation (4.17) and can be written as:

$$\frac{\partial Y}{\partial \lambda_1} = (1 - z)\frac{\partial X_2}{\partial \lambda_1} \tag{5.7}$$

By substituting (5.7) in (5.5) and on rearrangement of terms, we obtain:

$$\frac{\partial M_2}{\partial \lambda_1} = [m_h(1 - z) - 1]\frac{\partial X_2}{\partial \lambda_1} \tag{5.8}$$

By substituting (5.8) in (5.3), we finally obtain:

$$\frac{dp}{d\lambda_1} = \frac{[m_h(1 - z) - 1]\dfrac{\partial X_2}{\partial \lambda_1}}{[\epsilon_f + \epsilon_h - 1]M_2} \tag{5.9}$$

Equation (5.9) provides us with the expression that indicates the impact of technical progress on terms of trade. An interesting set of possibilities emerges from an examination of equation (5.9). Given stability conditions the sign of (5.9) depends exclusively on the sign of the numerator.

Let us first suppose that we are in the non-distortionary framework ($\mu = 1$). If $\mu = 1$, then from equation (4.17), it is obvious that $z > 1$; this is because $F_1 d\lambda_1$, the shift factor, is always positive. The imported good is assumed to be non-inferior in consumption, which implies that the marginal propensity to consume the imported good is positive and less than one ($0 < m_h < 1$). Since $z > 1$ it immediately follows that the bracketed expression in (5.9) is negative. Hence, the sign of $dp/d\lambda_1$ depends on $\partial X_2/\partial \lambda_1$. In the first best framework, Hicks-neutral technical progress in sector 1 always results in an expansion of sector 1 and a contraction in sector 2, hence, $(\partial X_2/\partial\lambda_1) < 0$. Since both terms in the numerator are negative and the denominator is positive, it follows that $(dp/d\lambda_1) > 0$, which implies that Hicks-neutral technical progress in the exporting sector always results in a deterioration in the terms of trade. This result occurs because technical progress causes an increase in the level of imports which is not matched by a movement in the output of the import-competing sector.

This standard result is presented geometrically in Figure 5.1, where TT is the pre-growth production possibility locus and TT' the post-growth production possibility locus. At constant terms of trade, in the

Figure 5.1

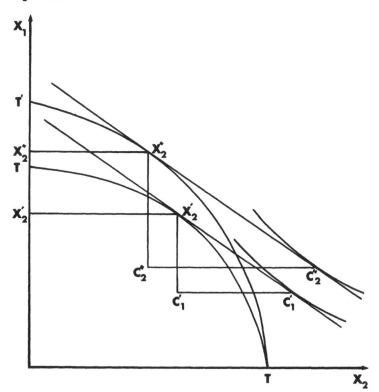

pre-growth equilibrium $X_2'X_2'$ of commodity 2 is produced domestically and $C_1'C_1'$ is imported from abroad. In the post-growth situation at constant terms of trade $X_2''X_2''$ of commodity 2 is produced and $C_2''C_2''$ of commodity 2 is required for imports. It is obvious from the diagram that $X_2''X_2'' < X_2'X_2'$ and $C_2''C_2'' > C_1'C_1'$, so at constant terms of trade the imports required rise, which ultimately lead to a deterioration in the terms of trade.

It is now appropriate to consider the impact of technical progress on terms of trade in the presence of a wage differential. The stability condition is again assumed to be satisfied, so that the denominator of (5.9) is positive. Our task again is the analysis of the sign of the numerator of (5.9), which consists of two terms $[m_h(1-z)-1]$ and $\partial X_2/\partial\lambda_1$. In the presence of the differential $z \gtrless 1$ and m_h is assumed to be $0 < m_h < 1$. Since m_h lies between zero and one, it immediately follows that irrespective of the value of z, the bracketed expression $[m_h(1-z)-1]$ is always negative. Hence, even in the distortionary framework and (given stability conditions) the movement in the terms of trade depends on the response of output of sector 2 to technical progress in sector 1. This response in the presence of distortions is ambiguous. We shall concentrate on the analysis of the non-standard case, namely the rise in the output of the non-progressive sector. From theorem 4.2, we know that the output of the non-progressive sector rises (in our case sector 2) if value-intensity reversals occur. Supposing that the conditions required for theorem 4.2 are satisfied, this implies that $(\partial X_2/\partial\lambda_1) > 0$. Hence, the numerator is negative and $(dp/d\lambda_1) < 0$, which implies that the terms of trade improve as a result of Hicks-neutral technical progress in sector 1. It is important to distinguish two cases here: (a) in which the output of sector 2 rises and sector 1 falls; and (b) in which both outputs rise, i.e. the output of exportables as well as importables rises. In both cases the terms of trade move in favour of the growing country. The latter case (b) has impact on the traditional Hicksian result that export-biased growth generally leads to a deterioration in the terms of trade.[4] The Hicksian result does not necessarily hold in the presence of distortions.

The intuitive explanation of the above result can be given quite easily with the help of diagrams. These diagrams clearly bring out the forces at work which cause the occurrence of the non-standard result.

In Figures 5.2 and 5.3 both cases are presented. A detailed explanation is only given for Figure 5.2. The interested reader can interpret Figure 5.3 easily. In Figure 5.2 TT is the pre-growth transformation locus and TT′ the post-growth transformation locus.

Figure 5.2

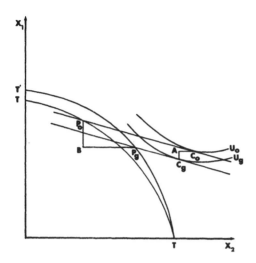

Figure 5.3

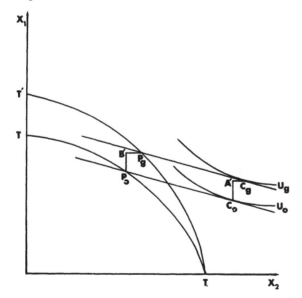

The pre-growth production equilibrium occurs at P_0 and consumption equilibrium at C_0. The welfare level is indicated by U_0. In the post-growth situation production equilibrium occurs at P_g and consumption equilibrium at C_g. The welfare level is indicated by U_g. Due to the perverse response of output to technical progress at constant terms of trade the level of output of the non-progressive sector rises by BP_g. Since U_g is, welfare-wise, lower than U_0, in other words welfare (income) falls due to growth, the demand for imports in the new equilibrium falls by C_0A. Hence, at constant terms of trade, the level of imports required falls, which ultimately leads to an improvement in the terms of trade. This result is caused by value-intensity reversals as well as 'immiserising growth'.

5.2 Factor Accumulation and Terms of Trade

It is now appropriate to examine the impact of factor accumulation on terms of trade. Since our model has two primary factors of production, labour (L) and capital (K), there are two sources of factor accumulation. Results for both types of accumulation are presented below.

The impact of factor accumulation on terms of trade can be derived by following the procedure used in the section on technical progress. Hence, the method used in arriving at the formal expressions can be omitted. The expressions indicating the impact of capital and labour accumulation on terms of trade are given below:

$$\frac{dp}{dK} = \frac{A}{(k_2 - k_1)[\epsilon_f + \epsilon_h - 1]M_2} \tag{5.10}$$

where

$$A = w_1[m_h(\mu - 1) - \mu] + rk_2[m_h - 1] - m_h k_1$$

$$\frac{dp}{dL} = \frac{B}{(k_2 - k_1)[\epsilon_f + \epsilon_h - 1]M_2} \tag{5.11}$$

where

$$B = (1 - m_h)\mu k_1 w_1 + rk_2 k_1 + m_h w_1 k_2$$

Equations (5.10) and (5.11) provide the formal expressions that indicate the impact of capital and labour accumulation on terms of trade.

The signs of (5.10) and (5.11) can be analysed very easily. In (5.10) A is always negative and, from stability conditions, $[\epsilon_f + \epsilon_h - 1]M_2$ always positive. Therefore, the impact of capital accumulation on terms of trade always depends on the ranking of sectors by physical intensities, $k_2 \gtrless k_1$, and $(dp/dK) \gtrless 0$ as $k_1 \gtrless k_2$. In other words, the terms of trade deteriorate (improve) depending on whether sector 1 is more (less) capital-intensive than sector 2. The explanation of this result is quite trivial. When $k_1 > k_2$, capital accumulation via the Rybczynski theorem results in an expansion of sector 1, the exporting sector, and a contraction of sector 2, the importing sector. Since the exporting sector expands, the terms of trade move against the growing country. This in fact is a standard and well known result and is not affected by the presence of a wage differential.

A similar analysis can be made of expression (5.11) indicating the impact of labour accumulation on terms of trade. The analysis does not lead to any new results. Thus the impact of factor accumulation on terms of trade even in the presence of a wage differential is the same as in the first best framework. This stands in sharp contrast with technical progress where standard results may not hold.

5.3 Economic Expansion and Real Income With Variable Terms of Trade

In the last two sections of the present chapter the consequences of economic expansion for terms of trade were analysed. These implications will now be utilised to adjust the change in real income for movements in the terms of trade. Economic expansion was subdivided into two sources: (a) technical progress; and (b) factor accumulation. We shall confine our treatment to technical progress only. This is because the two sources of expansion give rise to similar results, so treatment of one source is quite adequate.

Let us suppose that income is a function of the terms of trade and technical progress:

$$Y = Y(p, \lambda_1) \tag{5.12}$$

By differentiating equation (5.12) totally, we obtain:

$$\frac{dY}{d\lambda_1} = \frac{\partial Y}{\partial \lambda_1} + \frac{\partial Y}{\partial p} \cdot \frac{dp}{d\lambda_1} \tag{5.13}$$

Differentiation of national income equation with respect to p yields:

$$\frac{\partial Y}{\partial p} = \frac{\partial X_1}{\partial p} + X_2 + p \frac{\partial X_2}{\partial p} \tag{5.14}$$

With the help of equations (5.14) and (4.17), equation (5.13) can be transformed to:

$$\frac{dY}{d\lambda_1} = \frac{\partial Y}{\partial \lambda_1} + X_2[(1 - z)e + 1]\frac{dp}{d\lambda_1} \qquad (5.15)$$

where

$$e = \frac{p}{X_2} \cdot \frac{\partial X_2}{\partial p}$$

e is the elasticity of output of importables with respect to the relative price of importables. The sign of e is generally positive, although, in the presence of a wage differential, the sign can become negative. We shall, however, assume that the sign is positive. A number of results can be derived on the basis of equation (5.15), but we shall confine our attention to two results which seem to be rather interesting. These cases clearly bring out the nature of results that are obtainable for changes in real income at variable terms of trade.

Let us suppose that as a result of technical progress in sector 1 the terms of trade move against the growing country. This implies that $(dp/d\lambda_1) > 0$, i.e. technical progress results in an increase in the relative price of the importable commodity. It is further assumed that $\mu > 1$ and $z < 1$. Given these assumptions the bracketed term in equation (5.15) is positive, and hence the second term is positive. It also follows that both $\partial Y/\partial \lambda_1$ and $dY/d\lambda_1$ are positive. Since both terms on the right side of equation (5.15) are positive it follows immediately that $(dY/d\lambda_1) > (\partial Y/\partial \lambda_1)$. In other words, real income at variable terms of trade is greater than at constant terms of trade, despite the deterioration in the terms of trade resulting from technical progress. This strange result is due to the wedge created by the distortion between the production possibility locus and the commodity price ratio. This also shows an application of our result on terms of trade and welfare which shows that welfare may rise as a result of a deterioration in the terms of trade.

This result is presented diagrammatically in Figure 5.4. TT is the pre-growth production possibility locus, P_0 the pre-growth production point, T_0T_0 the pre-growth terms of trade, and U_0 the pre-growth welfare level. TT' is the post-growth production possibility locus, P'_c the post-growth production point and U'_c the post-growth welfare level at constant terms of trade. Now suppose the terms of trade deteriorate, denoted by the slope of T_vT_v. At the terms of trade T_vT_v the economy attains the welfare level $U_v > U'_c$. Note that the increase in welfare at constant terms of trade is less than at variable terms of trade even though the terms of trade have moved against the country. The diagram clearly reveals the forces at work which give rise to this non-

Figure 5.4

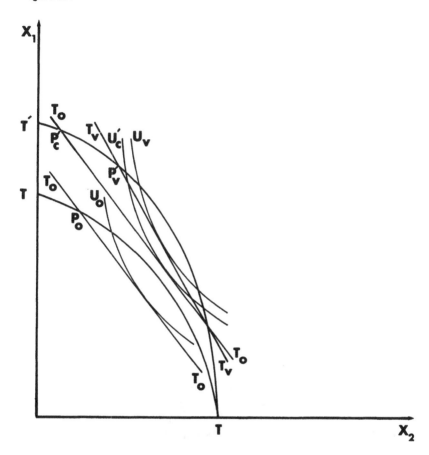

standard result. At constant terms of trade, production point moves from P_0 to P'_c – output of X_1 rises and X_2 falls. Let the terms of trade deteriorate. The deterioration in the terms of trade takes production from P'_c to P'_v, that is an increase in the output of X_2 and a decrease in the output of X_1. Hence, on the post-growth locus labour shifts from sector 1 to sector 2. Sector 2 pays a higher wage because $\mu > 1$, and hence this movement represents a productivity gain to the economy. This productivity gain may outweigh the consumption loss associated with an adverse movement in the terms of trade, giving rise to the possibility shown in Figure 5.4.

Let us now suppose that technical progress at constant terms of trade results in 'immiserising growth' which implies that in (5.15), $(\partial Y/\partial \lambda_1) < 0$. It is further supposed that $z < 1$ and that the terms of trade deteriorate. Given that $z < 1$ and $e > 0$ it follows that the second term in (5.15) is positive while the first term is negative. Therefore, the sign of real income at variable terms of trade is ambiguous. The most interesting case here is one in which the positive term is large and outweighs decline in income at constant terms of trade by so much that the economy ends up in a welfare position that is superior to both the original position as well as the post-growth situation at constant terms

Figure 5.5

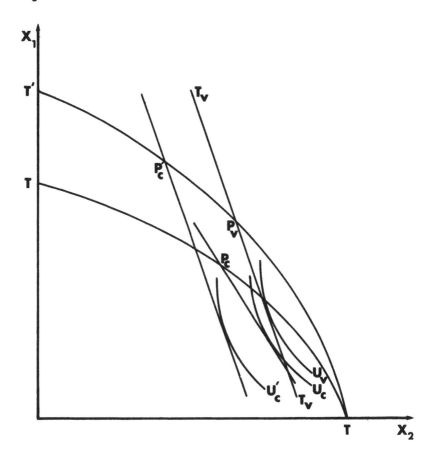

of trade.

This interesting possibility is presented geometrically in Figure 5.5 where TT is the pre-growth production possibility locus and TT′ the post-growth production possibility locus. In the pre-growth situation production occurs at P_c. The original welfare level is indicated by U_c. In the post-growth situation production takes place at P_c'. Welfare in the new situation is indicated by U_c'. Now $U_c' < U_c$, so, at constant terms of trade, 'immiserising growth' occurs. Now suppose the terms of trade deteriorate, indicated by the slope of the line $T_v T_v$. This takes production to P_v and welfare to U_v, which is greater than both the original welfare level as well as the post-growth welfare level at constant terms of trade ($U_v > U_c > U_c'$). This is indeed a very interesting result because in this case the deterioration in the terms of trade not only increases welfare but may be of such a magnitude as to wipe out 'immiserising growth'. This stands in sharp contrast to the result in the monopoly power in trade framework where a deterioration in the terms of trade may lead to 'immiserising growth'.[5]

5.4 Summary

We have completed our analysis of the impact of economic expansion on terms of trade and welfare (at variable terms of trade). It has been shown that the traditional view that export-biased growth generally results in a deterioration in the terms of trade of the growing country need not hold in the presence of a factor price differential. This result casts doubt on the theoretical underpinnings of the two hypotheses — the dollar problem and the secular deterioration of the terms of trade of less-developed countries.

It has also been shown in the present chapter that in contrast with the perfectly competitive model a deterioration (improvement) in the terms of trade may reduce (increase) 'immiserisation'. This is a consequence of the result that in the factor price differential case an improvement (deterioration) in the terms of trade may lower (raise) welfare.

Notes

1. A very lucid treatment of the method of comparative statics in international trade is available in Mundell (15).
2. Note that only M_2 has been made a function of λ_1. This is so because $E_1(p)$ is generated from the production and consumption structure of the foreign country which is not subject to technical progress. It is only at the point of equilibrium that the value of exports equals the value of imports.

3. See, for example, Bhagwati and Srinivasan (4).

4. The term export bias is being interpreted to imply that technical progress occurs in the exporting sector and at least leads to an increase in the output of the exporting sector.

5. See Bhagwati (2).

References

On Economic Expansion and Terms of Trade

(1) Bastable, C. F. 1903. *The Theory of International Trade*, 4th ed. London: Macmillan.

(2) Bhagwati, J. N. 1958. Immiserizing Growth: A Geometrical Note. *Review of Economic Studies*, Vol. 25 (June), 201–5.

(3) Bhagwati, J. N. 1958. International Trade and Economic Expansion. *American Economic Review*, Vol. 68 (December), 941–53.

(4) Bhagwati, J. N., and Srinivasan, T. N. 1971. The Theory of Wage Differentials: Production Response and Factor Price Equalisation. *Journal of International Economics*, Vol. 1 (February), 19–35.

(5) Corden, W. M. 1956. Economic Expansion and International Trade: A Geometrical Approach. *Oxford Economic Papers*, new series, Vol. 8 (June), 223–8.

(6) Edgeworth, F. Y. 1894. The Theory of International Values I. *Economic Journal*, Vol. 4 (March), 35–50.

(7) Edgeworth, F. Y. 1899. On a Point in the Pure Theory of International Trade. *Economic Journal*, Vol. 9 (March), 125–8.

(8) Findlay, R., and Grubert, H. 1959. Factor Intensity, Technological Progress and the Terms of Trade. *Oxford Economic Papers*, new series, Vol. 2 (February), 111–21.

(9) Hazari, B. R. 1975. Factor Market Distortions, Technical Progress and Trade. *Oxford Economic Papers*, new series, Vol. 27 (March), 47–60.

(10) Hicks, J. R. 1953. An Inaugural Lecture: The Long-Run Dollar Problem. *Oxford Economic Papers*, new series, Vol. 5 (June), 117–35.

(11) Johnson, H. G. 1958. *International Trade and Economic Growth*, Chapter III. London: George Allen and Unwin.

(12) Kemp, M. C. 1969. *The Pure Theory of International Trade and Investment*. Englewood Cliffs, New Jersey: Prentice-Hall.

(13) Mill, J. S. 1909. *Principles of Political Economy*, ed. Sir W. J. Ashley, Ch. III. London: Longmans Green.

(14) Prebisch, R. 1959. Commercial Policy in the Underdeveloped Countries. *American Economic Review*, Vol. 71 (May), 251–73.

General Reference

(15) Mundell, R. A. 1960. The Pure Theory of International Trade. *American Economic Review*, Vol. 50 (March), 67–110.

Part Two

MINIMUM WAGE RATES AND THE PURE THEORY OF INTERNATIONAL TRADE

6 MINIMUM WAGE RATES AND SOME PROPOSITIONS IN THE PURE THEORY OF TRADE

Trade theorists have been concerned with analysing the consequences of two types of factor market imperfections, namely (a) intersectoral differences in the reward of qualitatively identical factors and (b) the consequences of the existence of an exogenously specified minimum real wage. Part One of this critique has been devoted to an analysis of the implications of the first type of distortion for several propositions in the pure theory of international trade. It is now appropriate to discuss the consequences of the second type of distortion.

The presence of a factor price differential in the standard trade model does not create any unemployment. However, in the distortion of type (b), the specification of a real wage above the competitive level results in partial unemployment of the labour force. The *main* focus of attention in the minimum wage framework is generally the level of employment and welfare.

We shall consider two alternative specifications of the minimum wage. In this chapter the minimum (sticky) real wage is assumed to prevail in both sectors of the economy[1] and is taken to be specified exogenously. The real wage rate is, of course, assumed to be flexible in the upward direction. The problems of unemployment in such an economy only arise when market forces bid the level of real wages downward, such that the minimum wage becomes a binding constraint and remains at a level higher than the one required for attaining full employment.

We first rewrite the model of Chapter 1 to incorporate the minimum wage restriction. On the basis of the minimum wage model, the distorted production possibility locus is derived. We then proceed to discuss the welfare ranking of free trade *vis-à-vis* no trade. The level of employment associated with the two equilibrium positions is also discussed. The impact of an exogenous change in the terms of trade on welfare and employment is also analysed. Finally, the consequences of economic expansion on welfare and unemployment are discussed in the minimum wage economy.

6.1 The Model With a Minimum Wage

We now wish to introduce a minimum real wage in our two-sector economy. In order to do this the real wage is defined in the following manner:

$$\frac{1}{p}w_1 = w_2 \qquad (6.1)$$

where w_i denotes the real wage in terms of commodity i, and p is the relative price of the second good in terms of the first good. Given the assumption of profit maximisation, it follows that in equilibrium the reward for each factor equals its marginal product, hence:

$$w_i = f_i - k_i f_i' \qquad i = 1, 2 \qquad (6.2)$$

Each factor's reward will be assumed to be equal between sectors.

Equation (6.1) can be used to specify a minimum real wage, which is taken to be given exogenously. Since in the present model there are two goods X_1 and X_2, the minimum wage can be defined in three alternative ways: (i) the minimum wage specified in terms of X_1; (ii) the minimum wage specified in terms of X_2; and (iii) the minimum wage specified in terms of a utility combination of goods 1 and 2. We shall confine our discussion to (ii) only.[2]

Let $\bar{w}_2$ denote the exogenously specified minimum wage in terms of commodity 2.[3] Given this, the minimum wage constraint can be formulated as:

$$\frac{1}{p}w_1 = w_2 \geqslant \bar{w}_2 \qquad (6.3)$$

The imposition of the minimum real wage alters the shape of the supply curve for labour. In the non-distortionary model the supply curve of labour is inelastic as shown in Figure 6.1a. In the case of the minimum wage economy the supply curve of labour is perfectly elastic at the minimum wage until the full-employment level $\bar{L}$, where the curve assumes its traditional shape. This is shown in Figure 6.1b. Equilibrium occurs at the point where the demand curve for labour intersects the supply curve. If the intersection occurs to the left of the full-employment point (say A) then part of the labour force remains unemployed.

The market for capital is assumed to be non-distorted, and hence capital remains fully employed.

We are now in a position to derive various results relating to the minimum wage economy.

6.2 Production Possibility Curve in the Minimum Wage Economy

The production possibility curve relating to the minimum wage

Figure 6.1a

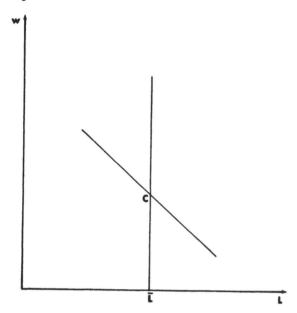

Figure 6.1b

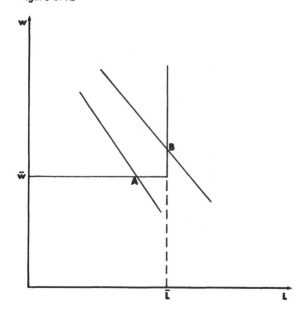

economy is derived on the basis of the conventional production possibility locus.[4] Two theorems play an important part in deriving the distorted locus: the Stolper–Samuelson theorem and the Rybczynski theorem. To derive the distorted locus, we start by recapitulating some features of the perfectly competitive economy.

Let us suppose that sector 1 is physically capital-intensive compared with sector 2 ($k_1 > k_2$) at all factor prices. Given the restriction on production functions in Chapter 1 and a fixed endowment of labour and capital, the unique concave to the origin production possibility curve can be generated.[5] This is shown as $T_0 T_0'$ in Figure 6.2. Suppose

Figure 6.2

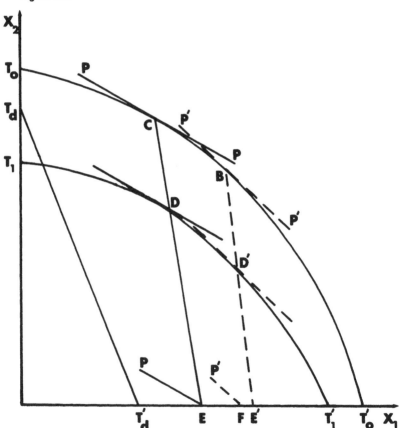

the relative price of good 1 is given by the slope of the line PP. Assuming profit maximisation, production occurs at point C in Figure 6.2. Associated with point C is an implicit factor price ratio. This factor price ratio is, of course, given by the slope of the line that is tangent to the two isoquants associated with point C in the Edgeworth–Bowley box diagram (not shown).

Let us suppose that a minimum real wage in both sectors is imposed exogenously (equation (6.3)). The minimum wage does not allow market forces to drive the wage level below the floor set by equation (6.3), and hence full employment does not necessarily occur in such an economy. However, capital remains fully employed because the market for capital is assumed to be perfectly competitive. Variation in employment, when parametric changes are made, only occur with regard to labour.

Suppose that the minimum wage in both sectors corresponds with the price ratio given by the slope of PP and production point C. Now consider an alternative production point on the transformation locus such as B in Figure 6.2. At B more of X_1 is produced and less of X_2. This implies that for production to occur at B the commodity price ratio must move in favour of X_1. Let this price ratio be given by the slope of P'P' in Figure 6.2. Since the relative price of good 1 rises at point B compared with C, it follows from the Stolper–Samuelson theorem that the real reward of the factor used intensively (non-intensively) rises (falls). Since X_1 is capital-intensive this implies that at B the reward of capital is higher and that of labour lower in comparison with point C. Since the minimum wage constraint was set at the wage level associated with point C, point B is no longer feasible. Using the Stolper–Samuelson argument, the real wage constraint is not satisfied at the points to the right of C (except the corner point) on the normal production possibility locus $T_0 T_0'$.

The question that arises naturally is: what is the shape of the production possibility locus at point C and to the right of point C? This can be derived readily by the use of the Rybczynski theorem. Consider a reduction in the labour force at constant prices. The capital stock is assumed to be given and remains fully employed. The reduction in the labour force gives rise to a new production possibility locus, $T_1 T_1'$. At constant prices production equilibrium on the new locus occurs at a point like D. Point D is admissible because at D the minimum wage constraint is satisfied. At D capital is fully employed but part of the labour force is unemployed. Points similar to D can be constructed by considering successive reductions in the labour force.

The locus of such points is given by CDE. The line CDE is known as the Rybczynski line.[6] Along CDE the wage constraint is satisfied because the prices are constant, and hence the wage–rental ratio is constant. Since we have chosen the initial sticky wage to be one associated with the slope of PP and the wage has not altered along CDE, it follows that CDE is part of the transformation locus. Along CDE unemployment is increasing. Labour is unemployed because at D output of X_1 has increased and X_2 decreased. Given constant prices, labour and capital are released in a constant proportion from X_2, which is labour-intensive compared with X_1. Hence the expansion of X_1 does not absorb all the labour released from X_2. Part of the released labour remains unemployed. It is also obvious from the diagram that due to the minimum wage constraint there are multiple production equilibria associated with the commodity price ratio given by the slope of PP. These of course can be eliminated by the introduction of demand conditions.

Consider an alternative price ratio given by the slope of P'P'. The slope of P'P' is greater than that of PP which implies that the relative price of good 1 has risen. From the Stolper–Samuelson argument it follows that the wage rate associated with P'P' is lower than the one associated with PP and therefore point B is inadmissible because it does not satisfy the minimum wage constraint. The Rybczynski line associated with point B is BD'E'. Since along BD'E' the wage is lower than the minimum wage we have postulated all points on BD'E' are inadmissible. Thus, incomplete specialisation is no longer possible, because at all production points associated with incomplete specialisation the minimum wage constraint is not satisfied.

Production equilibrium for prices given by the slope of P'P' occurs at the point of complete specialisation F. Point F is in fact unique. From our earlier arguments, we know that point E satisfies the minimum wage constraint. We also know that point E' does not satisfy minimum wage constraint for price level associated with the slope of P'P'. Point F is an equilibrium point for the price ratio given by the slope of P'P', because the relative price of good 2 has decreased from the original level indicated by the slope of PP, so unemployed labour at point E can now bid the wage down in terms of good 1. The change in the wage rate in terms of good 1 results in an increase in employment and output of good 1 from E to F. If the price ratio moves further in favour of commodity 1, then the new output point moves to the right of F and employment and output grow. There also exists a price ratio which will result in achieving full employment at point T_0'.

Points to the left of C on the transformation locus are all admissible because at those points the minimum wage constraint is non-binding. These points are all full-employment points. Thus, if the exogenously specified minimum wage is taken to be the one associated with the price level denoted by the slope of PP, the distorted production possibility curve is given by T_0CDEFT_0'.

If the minimum wage is raised beyond the level associated with the price level given by the slope of PP, then the price ratio for incomplete specialisation has also to be raised in favour of commodity 2. By raising the minimum wage rate sufficiently it can be seen, by the application of the technique outlined above, that the transformation curve becomes $T_dT_d'ET_0'$, as shown in Figure 6.3.[7] Only at T_0' can the economy attain a position of full employment.

Figure 6.3

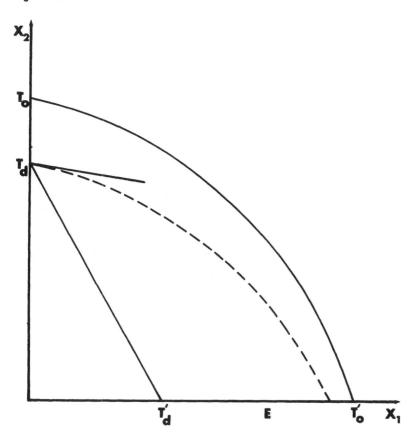

The differences between the first best model and the minimum wage economy are summarised below. In the non-distortionary framework both factors are fully employed. Given any price ratio and concavity of the production possibility schedule the production equilibrium is unique.[8] Changes in commodity price ratio result in changes in the factor price ratio, leaving employment to be constant at the full-employment level. In the minimum wage economy (assuming the sticky wage to be a binding constraint, at least for part of the transformation locus) full employment of labour is not necessarily assured. Given any commodity price ratio the production equilibrium need not be unique. Finally, changes in the commodity price ratio may leave the factor price ratio unchanged and alter the level of employment in the economy.

6.3 Free Trade versus No Trade

In this section, we examine the proposition that for a small country free trade is the optimal policy, in the context of our minimum wage economy.

Let us assume that the imposition of the minimum wage constraint leads to the production possibility curve TABT′ in Figures 6.4a and 6.4b. The minimum wage constraint is binding in the region AT′ of the non-distorted production possibility locus. Thus, it has not been assumed that the minimum wage is binding over the whole range of the production possibility curve.

Let the autarky equilibrium in Figure 6.4a occur at a, which is a point of full employment. Let us suppose that the foreign price ratio is indicated by the slope of line PP′. At the prices given by the slope of PP′ equilibrium cannot occur on the first best production possibility locus TT′. This is so because on the first best locus, with prices PP′, the minimum wage constraint is not satisfied. In terms of our earlier arguments, production equilibrium occurs at the point P_f in Figure 6.4a on the distorted production possibility locus. Consumption equilibrium occurs at C_f and the associated welfare level is indicated by U_f. It is obvious from the diagram that $U_f < U_a$, and hence, in welfare terms, free trade is worse than no trade. It should also be noted that the free-trade equilibrium is characterised by unemployment. It is also obvious from the diagram that free trade is not the optimal policy.

An interesting possibility is shown in Figure 6.4b. In this diagram, although free trade is welfare-wise better than no trade, the free-trade equilibrium is characterised by unemployment. Thus, from Figures 6.4a and 6.4b the following results emerge:

Figure 6.4a

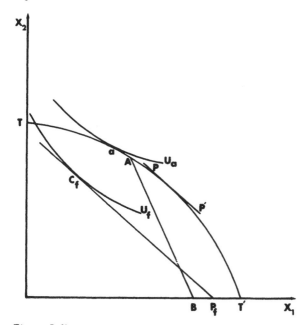

Figure 6.4b

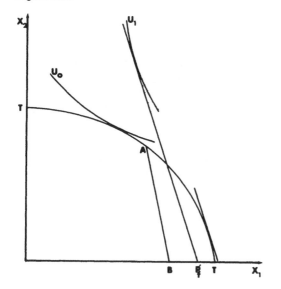

    (i) free trade cannot be ranked uniquely *vis-à-vis* no trade in the
        minimum wage economy;
   (ii) free trade is not the optimal policy in a minimum wage economy;
  (iii) a movement from no trade to free trade may be better than no
        trade in welfare terms but worse in terms of employment.

Point (iii) above indicates some of the problems associated with the use
of an aggregate utility function that only depends on the bundle of
goods actually consumed. Since employment falls as a consequence of
opening of model to trade, one may wish to use a social welfare
function that also takes into account society's welfare judgement about
unemployment. This particular problem is completely ignored in the
literature on minimum wages and trade.

    The optimal commercial policy for a small country is the removal of
the minimum wage constraint. The removal of the constraint will take
the economy to its first best locus where all the conditions for the
optimum solution will be satisfied.[9]

6.4 Terms of Trade, Employment and Welfare

We now seek to explore the relation between changes in the terms of
trade, employment and welfare. In the first best framework for a small
country an improvement (deterioration) in the terms of trade raises
(lowers) welfare. However, in the minimum wage economy changes in
the terms of trade not only have an impact on welfare but may also
change the level of employment in that economy.

    In Figures 6.5a and 6.5b we present the relation between changes in
the terms of trade, welfare and employment. Let us suppose that the
distorted production possibility locus is given by $TABT'$ and the
conventional production possibility locus by TT'. The minimum wage
is again assumed not to prevail over the entire production possibility
locus. This is done to bring into sharper focus the results obtained in
the minimum wage economy. In Figure 6.5a let the original terms of
trade be given by the slope of the line $P'P'$. Production equilibrium
occurs at P_0 and welfare is indicated by U_0. At the initial terms of
trade the economy is assumed to be in a position of full-employment
equilibrium and it exports X_1 and imports X_2. Supposing that an exogenous improvement in the terms of trade takes place, indicated by
the slope of the line $P'_I P'_I$, then production cannot occur on the conventional production possibility locus. By the analysis of section 6.2 on
the derivation of the distorted production possibility locus, production
occurs at the point of complete specialisation P'_I. Consumption is in-

Figure 6.5a

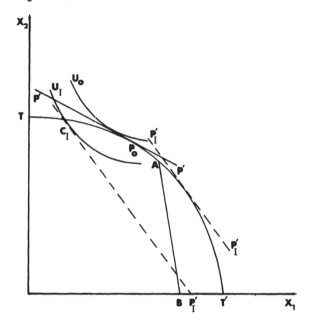

Figure 6.5b

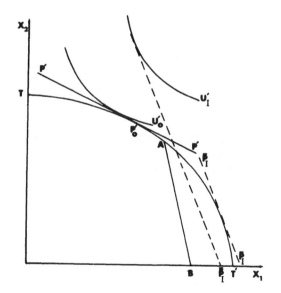

dicated by C_I and welfare by U_I. It follows immediately that an exogenous improvement in the terms of trade lowers welfare. Moreover, it takes the economy into a position of unemployment equilibrium.

Figure 6.5b illustrates the case in which an improvement in the terms of trade raises welfare but causes the economy to operate with partial unemployment of the labour force.

Thus in a minimum wage economy an improvement (deterioration) in the terms of trade may not raise (lower) welfare. Moreover, an improvement in the terms of trade may result either in creating unemployment or in accentuating unemployment or in decreasing unemployment (this case has not been analysed).

6.5 Economic Expansion, Employment and Welfare

Finally in this chapter, the impact of economic expansion on employment and welfare is considered. As indicated earlier, there are two sources of economic expansion in our model: (a) technical progress; and (b) factor accumulation. We shall only present results relating to technical progress.

Let us suppose that Hicks-neutral technical progress occurs in sector 1. The country is assumed to be small, i.e. the terms of trade are taken to be given exogenously. Let the conventional pre-growth production possibility curve in Figures 6.6a and 6.6b be given by TT_0. In Figure 6.6a it is assumed that the minimum wage constraint operates in the region aT_0 of the pre-growth transformation locus. Given the sticky wage constraint the distorted locus becomes $Taa'T_0$. If we suppose that the pre-growth production equilibrium occurs in the full-employment zone at P_0, then the pre-growth welfare level is given by U_a.

Technical progress in sector 1 leads to a shift in the production possibility locus. The normal production possibility locus shifts to TT_g. At constant prices, in the normal case production would have moved to P_g. Given $k_1 > k_2$ this implies that Hicks-neutral technical progress occurred in the capital-intensive sector. From equation (4.10) of Chapter 4, we know that for $\mu = 1$, the real wage falls as a consequence of neutral technical progress in the capital-intensive sector. It follows that at P_g the real wage is lower than at P_0. If this lowered wage rate does not satisfy the minimum wage constraint, then P_g is not an admissible production point.

Let the minimum wage requirement on the post-growth production possibility locus be satisfied at point $\bar{a}$. Now the new distorted locus will be $\bar{T}\bar{a}dT_g$. At constant terms of trade production equilibrium occurs at D. Welfare in the post-growth situation is indicated by U_g. Since

Figure 6.6a

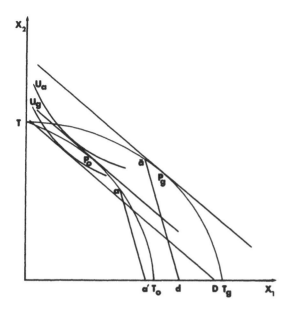

Figure 6.6b

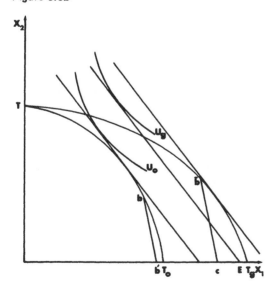

$U_g < U_a$ 'immiserising growth' occurs. Also note that at point D there is unemployment. Thus technical progress in sector 1 of a minimum wage economy may result not only in 'immiserising growth', but also in unemployment.

Results relating to factor accumulation can be derived in a similar fashion. These have been ignored as they do not provide any additional insights.

6.6 Summary

In this chapter, we have examined some consequences of the imposition of a minimum real wage constraint in both sectors of the economy. The specific results obtained are:

(1) Full employment is not necessarily assured in a model in which a minimum real wage constraint exists.

(2) In contrast with the fully competitive model, in a minimum wage economy, variations in prices may not result in variations in the wage—rental ratio but in variations in the level of employment.

(3) Free trade cannot be ranked uniquely *vis-à-vis* no trade in the presence of a minimum wage constraint.

(4) An improvement (deterioration) in the terms of trade may result not only in a loss (increase) in welfare, but also in increasing (decreasing) unemployment.

(5) Economic expansion may result not only in 'immiserising growth', but also in increasing unemployment.

Notes

1. In the following chapter (7) the wage is assumed to be sticky in only one sector of the economy. The wage in the second sector is equated with the expected wage rate. While the minimum wage specification in both sectors may result in general unemployment, the specification of a sticky wage (with an expected wage) leads to sectoral unemployment.

2. Brecher (2) in his masterly treatment of the theory of international trade under the minimum wage constraint discusses all the three specifications.

3. This specification of the minimum wage is related to the work of Bhagwati (1), Haberler (4) and Johnson (5). Haberler and Johnson do not specify the real wage exogenously. Both take the initial level of employment and wage as given. This initial wage is taken to be the minimum wage. Bhagwati sets exogenously the actual wage and rules out both upward and downward flexibility.

4. This can also be done on the basis of the Edgeworth–Bowley box diagram. However, the derivation based on the production possibility locus is much more elegant, and hence the choice of this technique. This technique was originally used by Brecher (2).

5. Different production possibility curves will correspond with different pairs of the labour (L) and capital (K) endowments.

6. The proof that the Rybczynski line is a straight line that slopes down to the right is available in Brecher (2), footnote 5, page 161.

7. Most results derived by Brecher (2) are based on this distorted linear transformation curve. In such a case the original equilibrium chosen is characterised generally by unemployment. The results established in this chapter do not depend on the assumption that the initial equilibrium chosen is one of full employment. They can be derived also for the case in which in the initial equilibrium there is some unemployment. This is exactly what Brecher does in his treatment of the problem.

8. If $k_1 = k_2$, then the production possibility locus is a straight line and multiple production equilibrium follows. Unique equilibrium is obtained by specifying the demand side of the model. A good treatment of the linear case ($k_1 = k_2$) is available in Batra (8).

9. Brecher (2) shows that this is not the optimal policy in the presence of monopoly power in trade.

References

On Minimum Wage Rates and the Pure Theory of International Trade

(1) Bhagwati, J. N. 1968. *The Theory and Practice of Commercial Policy.* Special Papers in International Economics, No. 8. Princeton.

(2) Brecher, R. 1971. Minimum Wage Rates and the Theory of International Trade. Unpublished doctoral dissertation, Harvard University.

(3) Brecher, R. 1974. Minimum Wages and the Theory of International Trade. *Quarterly Journal of Economics,* Vol. 88 (February), 98–116.

(4) Haberler, G. 1950. Some Problems in the Pure Theory of International Trade. *Economic Journal,* Vol. 60 (June), 223–40.

(5) Johnson, H. G. 1969. Minimum Wage Loss: A General Equilibrium Analysis. *Canadian Journal of Economics,* Vol. 2 (November), 599–604.

(6) Johnson, H. G., and Mieszkowski. 1970. The Effects of Unionization on the Distribution of Income: A General Equilibrium Approach. *Quarterly Journal of Economics,* Vol. 84 (November), 539–61.

(7) Lefeber, L. 1971. Trade and Minimum Wage Rates. In J. N. Bhagwati *et al.* (eds.), *Trade, Balance of Payments and Growth.* Amsterdam: North Holland.

On Multiplicity of Production Equilibria when $k_1 = k_2$

(8) Batra, R. N. 1973. *Studies in the Pure Theory of International Trade.* London: Macmillan.

7 SECTOR-SPECIFIC MINIMUM WAGES, URBAN UNEMPLOYMENT AND OPTIMAL COMMERCIAL POLICY IN A SMALL OPEN ECONOMY

In the preceding chapter, the consequences of introducing a minimum (sticky) wage in both sectors of the economy were analysed. We now consider an alternative specification of the minimum wage. This particular specification was introduced in the literature by Harris and Todaro (1970).[1] A minimum wage is introduced in only one sector of the economy, namely the manufacturing (urban) sector. The wage in the second sector – the agricultural (rural sector) is not set equal to the urban minimum wage, but is equated with the urban expected wage. The expected wage is defined as the sticky (minimum wage) weighted by the rate of employment in the manufacturing sector. The importance of the sticky wage specification in the manner of Harris–Todaro arises due to the light this model sheds on urban unemployment in less-developed countries. The model also shows why the traditional policy of subsidising labour in the urban sector is not the optimal policy.

The factor market imperfection created by specifying the minimum wage in the manner of Harris–Todaro differs from those discussed in Chapters 2–5 and in Chapter 6. In the model discussed in Chapters 2–5 there is no unemployment and it is the differential between the sectors that is held fixed in the analysis. In Chapter 6 there exists a sticky wage that prevails in both sectors of the economy leading to unemployment that is not specific to any sector. In the model presented in this chapter there is a minimum wage in the manufacturing (urban) sector. A differential exists between the manufacturing and agricultural sectors that depends on the expected wage rate. Thus this model combines specificity of wages in one sector with a wage differential in the other sector.

7.1 The Model With the Harris–Todaro Minimum Wage

The basic model that we shall employ is a variant of the two-sector model presented in Chapter 1. Since we wish to distinguish between the manufacturing (urban) sector and the agricultural (rural) sector, the model of Chapter 1 needs to be rewritten not only because the minimum wage constraint has to be introduced, but also due to the more specific labelling of the sectors.

Let us denote the aggregate utility function by:

$$U = U[C_A, C_M] \tag{7.1}$$

where U is assumed to be strictly concave and C_A and C_M denote the domestic consumption of agricultural and manufactured goods respectively.

From utility maximisation it follows:

$$\frac{U_A}{U_M} = \frac{P_A}{P_M} = p \tag{7.2}$$

where $U_i = \partial U/\partial C_i$ (i = A, M). This condition states that in equilibrium the marginal rate of substitution in consumption equals the ratio of prices.

It is assumed that part of the agricultural good is exported and part of the manufactured good is imported, so that:

$$C_A = X_A - E \tag{7.3}$$

$$C_M = X_M + I \tag{7.4}$$

where X_A and X_M denote the output of agricultural and manufactured goods. The term E denotes the export of the agricultural good and the term I the imports of the manufactured good.

The balance of payments equilibrium requires that the value of exports in equilibrium must equal the value of imports:

$$pE = I \tag{7.5}$$

The production functions of the two sectors are given by:

$$X_A = f_A(L_A, \bar{K}_A) \tag{7.6}$$

$$X_M = f_M(L_M, \bar{K}_M) \tag{7.7}$$

where L_i (i = A, M) indicates the allocation of labour to the ith sector The term $\bar{K}_A$ indicates the fixed capital stock utilised in agriculture and $\bar{K}_M$ the fixed capital stock utilised in the manufacturing sector. Thus capital is assumed to be immobile between the two sectors.[2] Both the production functions are assumed to be strictly concave.

Assuming profit maximisation the real wage rate in agriculture equals the value of its marginal product:[3]

$$w_A = pf'_A \tag{7.8}$$

The real wage in the manufacturing sector also equals the value of labour's marginal product in this sector (as in the agricultural sector) but is constrained by the sticky wage requirement:

$$w_M = f'_M \geqslant \bar{w}_M \tag{7.9}$$

This minimum wage is defined in terms of the manufactured good.[4]

It is now appropriate to define the urban expected wage:

$$w_u^e = \frac{\bar{w}_M L_M}{L_u}, \quad \frac{L_M}{L_u} \leqslant 1 \tag{7.10}$$

The expected real wage in the urban sector, w_u^e is equal to the real minimum wage $\bar{w}_M$ weighted by the total urban labour force actually employed, L_M / L_u (where L_u denotes the total urban labour force, that is, employed and unemployed labour). In other words, the expected wage is assumed to be equal to the average urban wage whenever $w_M = f'_M$. In the case of full employment in the manufacturing sector ($L_M = L_u$), that is, the expected wage equals the minimum wage.

Equilibrium condition requires that the real wage rate in the agricultural sector equals the expected wage rate:

$$w_A = w_u^e = \frac{\bar{w}_M L_M}{L_u} \tag{7.11}$$

This equilibrium condition is a by-product of the hypothesis that rural—urban migration is a positive function of the urban—rural expected wage differential.[5] Implicit in this migration function is the assumption that the migrant from the rural to the urban area gives up only his marginal product.

Finally, we have to introduce the labour constraint which states that:

$$L_A + L_u = \bar{L} \tag{7.12}$$

This equation implies that the sum of workers actually employed in agriculture (L_A) plus the total urban labour force (L_u) must equal the total labour endowment (L).

Given the assumption that the country is small, i.e. p is supplied exogenously, equations (7.1) to (7.12) give us a system of 12 equations in 12 unknowns: U, C_A, C_M, X_A, E, X_M, M, L_A, L_M, w_A, L_u and w_u^e. Once p and $\bar{w}_M$ are given, the system can be solved for the above-mentioned variables.

7.2 A Geometric Exposition of the Existence of Urban Unemployment in the Harris–Todaro Model

In the previous section we have described the structure of the Harris–Todaro model in a small open economy. Our first job is to demonstrate the existence of urban unemployment. This can be accomplished easily on the basis of simple geometry.[6]

In Figure 7.1 we measure along the horizontal axis the total endowment of the labour force. Point O_A represents the origin for labour employed in the agricultural (rural) sector and O_M the origin for labour employed in the manufacturing (urban) sector. Given the

Figure 7.1

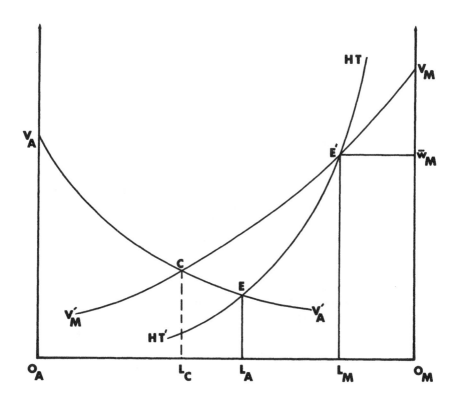

assumption that the country is small it is possible to draw the value of the marginal product curves for both sectors of the economy. Let $V_M V_M'$ and $V_A V_A'$ represent the value of marginal product curves for the manufacturing (urban) and agricultural (rural) sectors respectively. In the non-distortionary framework, we know from Chapter 1 that in equilibrium the value of marginal product in one sector must equal the value of marginal product in the other sector. In terms of Figure 7.1 the two values are equal at point C. $O_M L_C$ of the labour force is employed in manufacturing and $O_A L_C$ in agriculture, in the fully competitive framework labour is fully employed at the wage rate CL_C.

Let us introduce the exogenously specified wage w_M in the urban sector. Given the assumption of profit maximisation labour market equilibrium in the urban sector occurs at point E' where the value of the marginal product equals the sticky wage rate. Quantity $O_M L_M$ of the total labour force is employed in the manufacturing sector. We now have to decide on the allocation of the rest of the labour force $O_A L_M$. This part of the labour force can be allocated by drawing the Harris–Todaro curve in Figure 7.1,[7] which is the rectangular hyperbola HT HT'. The curve HT HT' is the geometrical representation of equation (7.11) which states that $w_A = L_M \bar{w}_M / L_u$. It intersects the value of the marginal product curve of the agricultural sector at point E, at which point the rural wage rate not only equals the value of marginal product in the agricultural sector but also the expected urban wage rate. Given the equilibrium point E, $O_A L_A$ is the labour employed in agriculture and $L_A L_M$ is the labour force that remains unemployed in the urban sector. The policy question that emerges from the above analysis is: what alternative policies can be used in the Harris–Todaro model to combat the problem of urban unemployment?[8]

7.3 Policy of Laissez-Faire

In this section, we examine the result that for a small country free trade is the optimal policy, in the presence of a Harris–Todaro type minimum wage restriction.

In Figure 7.2, TT' is the normal production possibility locus. Given the foreign price ratio production equilibrium occurs at point P and consumption equilibrium at point C. The level of welfare is indicated by U. Thus, in the non-distorted model the marginal rate of substitution in consumption equals the foreign rate of transformation which in turn equals the domestic rate of transformation.

The sector-specific rigid wage *à la* Harris–Todaro can be easily introduced into Figure 7.2. Let the free-trade solution above (at P and C

Figure 7.2

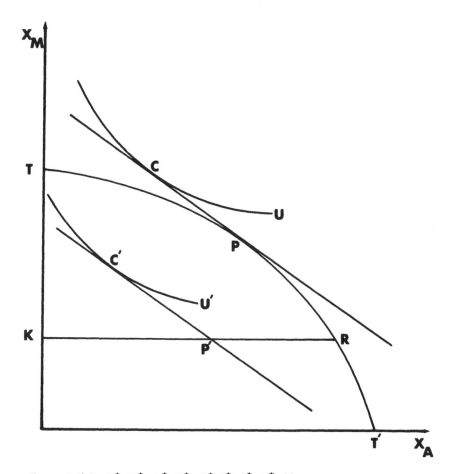

in Figure 7.2) be X_A^*, X_M^*, L_A^*, L_M^*, E^*, I^*, C_A^*, C_M^*. Now suppose we have the Harris–Todaro type minimum wage constraint, so that

$$f_M' \geqslant \bar{w}_M$$

Suppose the constraint on the wage rate becomes binding at point P in Figure 7.2, i.e.

$$f_M'(L_M^*) < \bar{w}_M$$

Obviously point P is inadmissible.

Given the binding wage constraint and our assumption that the agricultural wage rate equals the expected urban wage, equilibrium production under the policy of *laissez-faire* can lie only along RK (excluding R). The solution for L_A and L_M can be obtained from equations (7.6), (7.7), (7.9) and (7.10). Point R is inadmissible because it does not satisfy the constraints of the model. Production equilibrium now occurs at point P′ and consumption equilibrium at point C′. The welfare level is indicated by U′. This situation is characterised by two features, namely (a) the suboptimality of the policy of *laissez-faire* and (b) the presence of unemployment. In the case of factor price differential only (a) occurs. We shall analyse three policies: (a) wage subsidy in manufacturing;[9] (b) production subsidy in agriculture; and (c) a uniform wage subsidy. It will be assumed that all subsidies are financed by non-distortionary taxes and that there are no collection costs of taxes or disbursement cost of subsidies.

7.4 Wage Subsidy in Manufacturing

This section is devoted to the analysis of giving a wage subsidy in the manufacturing (urban) sector for welfare and employment. Let s be the wage subsidy in the manufacturing sector. This implies that in equilibrium the following condition must hold:

$$f'_M = \bar{w}_M - s \tag{7.13}$$

This equation replaces (7.9).

By using the procedure outlined earlier in the book the change in welfare due to a wage subsidy in the manufacturing sector is given by the following expression:

$$\frac{1}{U_M}\frac{dU}{ds} = p\frac{dX_A}{ds} + \frac{dX_M}{ds} \tag{7.14}$$

The solutions for dX_i/ds (i = A, M) can be obtained by using equations (7.6), (7.7), (7.11), (7.12) and (7.13). These are given below:

$$\frac{dX_A}{ds} = -\frac{f'_A}{f''_M}\left[\frac{\bar{w}_M}{(L_u f''_A - f'_A)}\right] \tag{7.15}$$

$$\frac{dX_M}{ds} = -\frac{f'_M}{f''_M} \tag{7.16}$$

By substituting (7.15) and (7.16) in (7.14), we obtain:

$$\frac{1}{U_M}\frac{dU}{ds} = \left[\frac{\bar{w}_M}{L_u f''_A - f'_A} + f'_M\right]\frac{dL_M}{ds} \tag{7.17}$$

Figure 7.3a

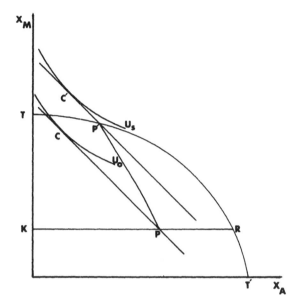

Figure 7.3b

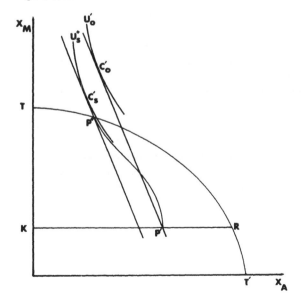

where

$$\frac{dL_M}{ds} = -\frac{1}{f_M''} > 0$$

Equation (7.17) provides us with the expression that indicates the change in welfare as a consequence of giving a wage subsidy in the manufacturing sector. The sign of $(1/U_M)(dU/ds)$ is ambiguous, because the bracketed expression in (7.17) does not possess a unique sign. The first term in the bracketed expression is negative, while the second term is positive. Hence, a subsidy in the manufacturing sector does not necessarily raise welfare.

An intuitive explanation of this result follows from an examination of equations (7.14), (7.15) and (7.16). Equation (7.14) shows that at constant prices the change in welfare depends on the movement in the output of the two sectors. Equations (7.15) and (7.16) show that as a result of the subsidy in the manufacturing sector the output of the manufacturing sector rises and that of the agricultural sector falls. Hence, welfare rises (falls) if the increase in the output of the manufacturing sector is greater (less) than the decrease in the output of the agricultural sector.

The increase in output of the manufacturing sector leads to more employment in the urban area. As s is increased, the level of employment rises and ultimately the economy moves to a full-employment equilibrium. However, this full-employment equilibrium need not be welfare-wise better than the *laissez-faire* equilibrium. Therefore, the trade-off possibilities between increased welfare and reduced unemployment may be very important if a wage subsidy is used as a policy measure in the urban sector.

In Figures 7.3a and 7.3b the above-mentioned cases are presented diagrammatically. In 7.3a the initial free-trade equilibrium occurs at P. Consumption takes place at point C and the welfare is indicated by U_0. The curve PP' is the locus of production equilibria traced out by increasing the wage subsidy in manufacturing from s = o to s max yielding full employment at P'. Consumption equilibrium occurs at point C' and welfare is indicated by U_s. Now $U_s > U_0$, and hence the free-trade equilibrium is welfare-wise worse than the full-employment equilibrium at P'. The inferiority of the full-employment equilibrium (with subsidy in the urban sector) compared with the free-trade equilibrium is illustrated in Figure 7.3b. It is obvious from Figures 7.3a and 7.3b that a wage subsidy in the manufacturing sector is not the optimal policy.

7.5 Production Subsidy to Agriculture

The policy of giving a production subsidy in the agricultural sector obviously leads to a modification of the equilibrium condition. This can be expressed as:

$$\pi_p f_A' = \frac{\bar{w} L_M}{L_u} \tag{7.18}$$

where π_p is the producer's price for the agricultural good. The production subsidy is indicated by $(\pi_p - p)/p$. We shall also assume that $f_M' = \bar{w}_M$, i.e. the wage constraint to be strictly binding.

We are again interested in asking two questions: (a) can the production subsidy restore full employment and (b) what happens to welfare as a result of the production subsidy to agriculture? The answers to these questions can again be obtained by deriving expressions of the type (7.14) to (7.17). These expressions are given below:

$$\frac{1}{U_M} \frac{dU}{d\pi_p} = - \frac{p f_A'}{[\pi_p L_u f_A'' - \pi_p f_A']} \tag{7.19}$$

$$\frac{dX_A}{d\pi_p} = - \frac{f_A'}{[\pi_p L_u f_A'' - \pi_p f_A']} \tag{7.20}$$

$$\frac{dX_M}{d\pi_p} = 0 \tag{7.21}$$

It follows trivially from equations (7.19) and (7.20) that both welfare and output of the agricultural sector rise as a consequence of a production subsidy in the agricultural sector. Equation (7.21) shows that a production subsidy in agriculture leaves the output of the urban sector completely undisturbed. The explanation of the unambiguous rise in welfare in this particular case is quite simple. Output of manufactures remains at the old level, agricultural output rises as a result of the production subsidy; hence total output increases. If the total output increases, then welfare must rise. Since the production subsidy results in an increase in agricultural output without a decrease in manufacturing output, it must result in a reduction in unemployment. It follows that there exists a production subsidy to agriculture that leads to full employment. However, this subsidy is not the optimal policy.

The above-mentioned result is presented diagrammatically in Figure 7.4, where TT' represents the normal production possibility locus. Equilibrium due to the minimum wage restriction cannot occur on TT'

Figure 7.4

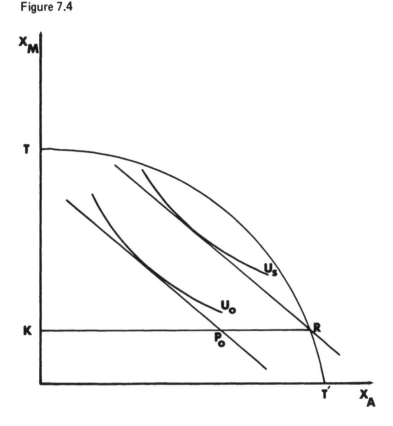

and only takes place on KR (excluding R). Suppose the initial production equilibrium occurs at P_0. Associated with P_0 is the welfare level U_0. A production subsidy to agriculture moves the economy along P_0R. The full-employment production subsidy leads to equilibrium at R. The welfare level associated with point R is U_s, and $U_s > U_0$. Since the movement is along P_0R all points are successively welfare-increasing for movements from P_0 to R. It is obvious from Figure 7.4 that a full-employment production subsidy to agriculture is not the optimal policy. It should be pointed out here that the policy of a wage subsidy in the manufacturing sector cannot be ranked *uniquely* in welfare terms *vis-à-vis* the policy of a production subsidy to the agricultural sector.

In Figures 7.5a and 7.5b we present the result that a full-employment

Figure 7.5a

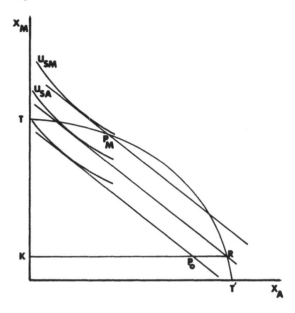

Figure 7.5b

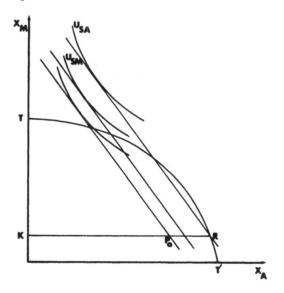

generating subsidy to the manufacturing sector cannot be uniquely ranked *vis-à-vis* a full-employment generating subsidy in the agricultural· sector.[10] In Figure 7.5a the full-employment generating subsidy to the manufacturing sector leads to production at P_M and welfare to U_{SM}. In the case of subsidising agriculture, production occurs at point R and welfare is indicated by U_{SA} and $U_{SM} > U_{SA}$. Hence, in Figure 7.5a, a production subsidy in the manufacturing sector is welfare-wise better than a production subsidy in the agricultural sector. The converse result is presented in Figure 7.5b.

7.6 Uniform Wage Subsidy (Optimal Policy Intervention)

In the last two sections we have shown that a wage subsidy to the urban sector and a production subsidy to the agricultural sector are not optimal policies. We have also shown while the latter policy always raises welfare, the welfare consequences of the former policy are ambiguous. Finally, we indicated that these policies cannot be ranked uniquely in welfare terms *vis-à-vis* each other.

It is now appropriate to consider the first best policy. The first best solution requires that labour allocation should be such that (i) there is no unemployment and (ii) the Paretian condition of equality of the value of marginal products in the two sectors be met.

The first best solution can be obtained by an equal wage subsidy in both sectors. Let

$$s^* = \bar{w}_M - f'_M(L_M^*)$$

be the wage subsidy in the urban sector. The asterisks indicate first best values. Since this subsidy is to be given to the agricultural sector also, the equilibrium conditions are:

$$f'_M = \bar{w}_M - s^*$$

$$pf'_A = \bar{w}_M - s^*$$

It is obvious that all the constraints of the model are met and the first best solution is reached with a uniform wage subsidy in both sectors.

In Figure 7.6 the first best solution is shown. This occurs at point P_s on the first best locus. At P_s all the conditions for the first best solution are satisfied.

7.7 Summary

This chapter has been devoted to a discussion of the consequences of a minimum real wage specification *à la* Harris–Todaro. We have shown

Figure 7.6

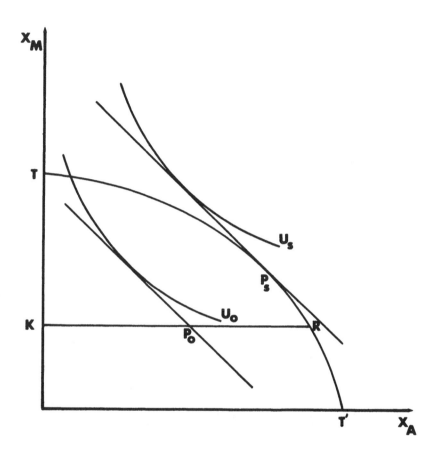

how this wage specification results in urban unemployment in less-developed countries. This model also highlights the fact that a policy involving a wage subsidy in the sector in which there is factor price rigidity is not the optimal policy. This conclusion runs counter to the traditional wisdom on the subject which tells us that a subsidy to the factor of which the price is rigid is an optimal policy. It has also been shown that free trade is not the optimal policy. The optimal policy is a wage subsidy in both sectors. This chapter also highlights the conflict between welfare and employment. A policy that raises employment need not necessarily raise welfare (welfare being dependent on the bundle of goods consumed). Hence, there exist trade-off possibilities between welfare and unemployment.

Notes

1. Harris and Todaro (7) set up a model with the sticky wage specification for a closed economy. The closed economy model is slightly more complex than one set up for a small open economy. The latter assumption allows one to take the prices to be given exogenously, thereby leading to the elimination of all expressions that involve a change in the prices of final goods.
2. Corden and Findlay (5) relax the assumption of specificity with regard to the stock of capital used in the agricultural and the manufacturing sectors.
3. Note that it is being assumed that labour in the agricultural sector earns its marginal product. This assumption ignores disguised unemployment. Many less-developed countries are characterised by disguised unemployment in the rural sector.
4. The minimum wage is specified in terms of the manufactured good. It could alternatively be specified either in terms of the agricultural good or in terms of a utility combination of agricultural and manufactured goods. The wage specification in terms of the manufactured good is a simplifying assumption and has no bearing on the main results of the present chapter. Harris and Todaro (7) present results also for the case in which the sticky wage is specified in terms of the agricultural good.
5. Harris and Todaro specify the migration function explicitly in the following manner:

$$\dot{L}_M = \psi \left[\frac{\bar{w}_M L_M}{L_u} - p f_A' \right]$$

$$\psi' > 0, \psi(0) = 0$$

where $\dot{L}_u$ is a time derivative. Migration ceases when the expected income differential is zero, the condition stated in equation (7.11). The main feature of the Harris–Todaro argument is that rural–urban migration brings the agricultural wage into equality with the expected wage. Unemployment in this framework is inevitable only if it is assumed that labour will not prefer certain employment at a lower wage in the agricultural sector to uncertain employment in the manufacturing sector at a higher wage. The Harris–Todaro specification assumes a random turnover in the manufacturing labour force, i.e. each member of the total urban labour force having an equal chance of being employed.
6. The geometrical technique used here is adopted from the exceedingly lucid treatment of the Harris–Todaro model provided by Corden and Findlay (5).
7. The labelling Harris–Todaro curve was also introduced by Corden and Findlay (5).
8. While the Corden–Findlay diagram is very useful in portraying urban unemployment, it is not very elegant for carrying out welfare analysis. Hence, in the following section we switch to the traditional diagrams, namely the production possibility curves and social indifference curves.
9. The examination of the consequences of a subsidy in the manufacturing sector is important because it is argued on the basis of the orthodox wage-differentials model that the first best policy is a wage subsidy in the manufacturing sector.

10. This result is not surprising in view of the Lipsey–Lancaster theorem which shows that two suboptimal points cannot be ranked uniquely.

References

(1) Bhagwati, J. N., and Srinivasan, T. N. 1974. On Reanalysing the Harris–Todaro Model: Policy Rankings in the Case of Sector-Specific Sticky Wages. *American Economic Review*, Vol. 64 (June), 502–8.
(2) Bhagwati, J. N., and Srinivasan, T. N. 1973. The Ranking of Policy Interventions Under Factor Market Imperfections: The Case of Sector-Specific Sticky Wages and Unemployment. *Sankhya*, Ser. B.
(3) Bhagwati, J. N., and Srinivasan, T. N. 1975. Alternative Policy Rankings in a Large, Open Economy with Sector-Specific Minimum Wages. *Journal of Economic Theory*, Vol. II (December), 356–71.
(4) Brecher, R. 1974. Minimum Wages Rates and the Theory of International Trade. *Quarterly Journal of Economics*, Vol. 88 (February), 98–116.
(5) Corden, W. M., and Findlay, R. 1975. Urban Unemployment, Intersectoral Capital Mobility and Development Policy. *Economica*, Vol. 42 (February), 59–78.
(6) Haberler, G. 1950. Some Problems in the Pure Theory of International Trade. *Economic Journal*, Vol. 60 (June), 223–40.
(7) Harris, J. R. and Todaro, M. P. 1970. Migration, Unemployment and Development: A Two Sector Analysis. *American Economic Review*, Vol. 60 (March), 126–42.

On the Second Best Theorem

(8) Lipsey, R. G., and Lancaster, K. 1957. The General Theory of the Second Best. *Review of Economic Studies*, Vol. 24 (February), 11–32.

Part Three

**EXTERNALITIES AND THE PURE THEORY OF
INTERNATIONAL TRADE**

8 MEADE-TYPE PRODUCTION EXTERNALITIES AND SOME PROPOSITIONS IN THE PURE THEORY OF TRADE

In the preceding six chapters, we have analysed the consequences of factor market imperfections for the pure theory of international trade. The product markets so far have been assumed to be perfect. It is now appropriate to discuss the implications of imperfections in the product market for trade theory, assuming that there are no imperfections in the factor market. The results obtained by the introduction of product market imperfection are compared with those obtained with factor market imperfections. Such a comparison highlights the difference in the impact of two different kinds of distortions, namely factor market imperfections *vis-à-vis* product market imperfections. We shall analyse the consequences of two types of product market imperfections: (a) the presence of a Meade-type production externality; and (b) the presence of a domestic monopoly. The present chapter is devoted to the considerations of the former product market imperfection while the consequences of the latter imperfection are analysed in Chapter 9.

Non-market interdependence among various economic agents is known as technical external economies and diseconomies. Technical external economies (diseconomies) are defined as the favourable (unfavourable) non-market effects, i.e. free (uncompensated) effects on one economic agent on another economic agent. For instance, the actions of a particular firm may influence the production functions of other firms. Similarly, the consumption activities of a particular consumer may affect the utility function of another consumer in the economy. Many other examples of the existence of externalities can easily be given.

We have already remarked that there are many types of externalities and naturally there are various economic and mathematical formulations to deal with these externalities. However, in this chapter we shall confine ourselves to discussing the impact of one specific type of externality – the Meade-type production externality on some propositions in the pure theory of trade.[1] Given the existence of this type of externality we shall examine (a) the optimality or non-optimality of the policy of free trade; (b) the relationship between terms of trade and welfare; (c) the Rybczynski theorem; (d) the

impact of economic expansion on welfare; and (e) the impact of
economic expansion on the expanding country's terms of trade. The
results obtained in this framework are compared with those obtained
in the framework of factor market imperfections.

8.1 The Model With Meade-Type Production Externality

Meade-type production externality can easily be introduced via the
production functions. The modified functions are given below:

$$X_1 = F_1(K_1, L_1) \tag{8.1}$$

$$X_2 = F_2(K_2, L_2, X_1) \tag{8.2}$$

where K_i, L_i stand for the amount of capital and labour employed in
the ith industry. The production function for commodity 2 depends not
only on K_2 and L_2 but also on the output of commodity X_1.[2] We
assume that F_1 is linear homogeneous in L_1 and K_1 and F_2 to be linear
homogeneous in L_2, K_2 and X_1.

Given the homogeneity assumption the production functions in
(8.1), (8.2) can be written in the intensive form:

$$X_1 = F_1(K_1, L_1) = L_1 f_1(k_1) \tag{8.3}$$

$$X_2 = F_2(K_2, L_2, X_1) = L_2 f_2(k_2, \bar{x}_1) \tag{8.4}$$

where k_i's denote the capital-intensity of the sectors and $\bar{x}_1$ denotes the
impact of the externality on sector 2 expressed in terms of labour
employed in sector 2.

Presented above are the equations that need to be changed by the
presence of Meade-type production externality. The rest of the
equations in Chapter 1 remain unaltered. We are now in a position to
derive results in the presence of the externality.

8.2 The Shape and the Slope of the Production Possibility Curve

Given the assumptions of profit maximisation and perfectly
competitive markets it is known that the firms pay the factors the value
of their marginal product. The presence of a Meade-type production
externality does not alter this particular property of the competitive
system and the factors of production continue to receive the value of
their marginal product. Since both sectors face the same wage–rental
ratio, in equilibrium they both have the same marginal rate of factor
substitution. Hence it follows that the position of the production
possibility curve is not affected by the presence of a Meade-type

production externality. Thus, in contrast to the single factor price differential case, where the economy operates on the inferior locus, in the case of a production externality the economy operates on the normal production possibility curve.[3]

The presence of the Meade-type production externality, however, affects the relationship between the production possibility curve and the commodity price ratio. In fact this type of externality creates a wedge between the production possibility curve and the commodity price ratio. A formal proof of this result is presented below. By differentiating the production functions totally, we obtain:

$$\frac{dX_1}{dX_2} = \frac{\frac{\partial X_1}{\partial L_1} dL_1 + \frac{\partial X_1}{\partial K_1} dK_1}{\frac{\partial X_2}{\partial L_2} dL_2 + \frac{\partial X_2}{\partial K_2} dK_2 + \frac{\partial X_2}{\partial X_1} dX_1}$$

From the factor endowment conditions, $dL_1 = -dL_2$ and $dK_1 = -dK_2$ and from the factor rewards condition we also know that $w = \partial X_1/\partial L_1$, $r = \partial X_1/\partial K_1$, $w/p = \partial X_2/\partial K_2$ and $r/p = \partial X_2/\partial K_2$. By appropriate substitutions and manipulation it follows that:

$$\frac{dX_1}{dX_2} = -\frac{p}{\theta} \tag{8.5}$$

where $\theta = (1 - b)$ and $b = p(\partial X_2/\partial X_1)$, θ is always positive. It is obvious from equation (8.5) that in equilibrium the slope of the production possibility locus does not equal the ratio of commodity prices. This occurs due to the presence of the externality which is indicated by the term b. Term b positive indicates that sector 1 is the source of an external economy for sector 2, while b negative indicates that sector 1 confers an external diseconomy on sector 2. Since $(1 - b)$ is positive it follows immediately from (8.5) that $\theta \gtrless 1$ as $b \lessgtr 0$.

It is also clear from equation (8.5) that $dX_1/dX_2 \gtrless p$ as $\theta \lessgtr 1$. This implies that at the position of equilibrium the slope of the production possibility locus is greater (less) than the commodity price ratio in the presence of an external economy (diseconomy). In Figures 8.1a and 8.1b both the possibilities are presented diagrammatically. In Figure 8.1a TT' represents the normal production possibility locus. Let us suppose that the economy is characterised by the presence of an external economy, i.e. $b > 0$ and $\theta < 1$. If $\theta < 1$, then in equilibrium the slope of the production possibility curve is greater than the commodity price ratio. Equilibrium occurs at a point like E where

Figure 8.1a

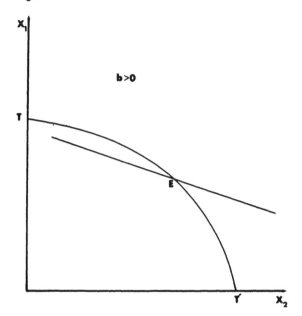

Figure 8.1b

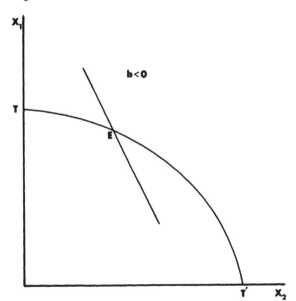

the commodity price ratio cuts the production possibility curve from below. At E the output of X_2 is more than is socially desirable due to the presence of an external economy. Figure 8.1b shows the case in which the system is characterised by the existence of an external diseconomy. Thus at the point of equilibrium the domestic rate of transformation does not equal the domestic rate of substitution which equals the foreign rate of transformation (DRS = FRT $\neq$ DRT).

The presence of a Meade-type production externality has only one structural effect – the non-tangency between the production possibility locus and the commodity price ratio. This is in contrast with the factor price differential case, where such differentials may lead to three consequences: (a) shrinkage of the production possibility locus; (b) breakdown of the ranking of sectors in the physical and value sense; and (c) non-tangency between the production possibility locus and the price line. Thus, the factor price differential case is more complex than the case of a production externality. The former distortion gives rise to various structural effects that are not logically possible in the case of a Meade-type production externality.[4]

8.3 Free Trade versus No Trade

In this section we consider the proposition that under the first best assumptions free trade is the optimal commercial policy. This policy conclusion is examined in the presence of a Meade-type production externality.

The policy of *laissez-faire* is defined as a situation in which the international price of commodities is the same as the domestic price of commodities. In order to prove the optimality or otherwise of the policy of *laissez-faire*, we follow the same procedure as the one used in Chapter 3, i.e. we examine the expression for a change in welfare given the initial position of free trade. This gives us the following expression for change in welfare:

$$\frac{dU}{U_1} = dX_1 + pdX_2 \tag{8.6}$$

By substituting from equation (8.5), equation (8.6) can be written as:

$$dU = U_1\left[\frac{\theta - 1}{\theta}\right]pdX_2 \tag{8.7}$$

There exist three possible values for θ in equation (8.7), $\theta = 1$, $\theta > 1$ and $\theta < 1$. In the first best framework θ equals one while in the presence of an externality θ is not equal to one. The first best result follows immediately when θ is set equal to one in 8.7.[5] Since in the presence of an externality θ is not equal to one, it follows immediately from equation (8.7) that $dU \neq 0$ and, therefore, free trade is not the optimal policy in the presence of a Meade-type production externality. This result is similar to the result contained in theorem 3.2. However, the reasons that cause *laissez-faire* to be a suboptimal policy in the presence of an externality are different from those that exist in the factor price differential case. This is explained via the use of diagrams.

In Figures 8.2a and 8.2b we present two cases, one in which free trade is better than no trade and the other in which free trade is worse than no trade. In both cases free trade is not the optimal policy. We shall discuss the case presented in Figure 8.2b, leaving the interpretation of 8.2a to the reader. In 8.2b, TT′ represents the normal production possibility locus. On this normal locus the autarky equilibrium occurs at point S, where the domestic price ratio given by the slope of line $P_d P_d$ cuts the transformation curve from above. The welfare level is indicated by U_s. Now consider the opening of trade. Given the assumption of free trade the international price ratio is given by the slope of line $P_b P_b$, which also becomes the domestic price ratio. This price ratio takes the production equilibrium to P_F and consumption equilibrium to C_F. The welfare level is indicated by U_F which is less than U_s. Free trade results in an increase in the output of X_1 and a decrease in the output of X_2. However, in the self-sufficiency situation X_1 is already being over-produced due to the presence of an externality. Free trade further accentuates the production loss arising due to an externality leading to the welfare result that free trade turns out to be worse than no trade. This production loss outweighs any consumption gain that may accrue to the economy as a result of opening of trade. It is precisely this that happens in Figure 8.2b, which not only shows that free trade is a suboptimal policy but also clearly indicates that free trade may be worse than a position of autarky.

Since we have established the suboptimality of the policy of *laissez-faire* the natural question to ask is what is the optimal policy? The answer to this question can be derived from the following expression:

$$dU = U_1 \left(\frac{\theta - 1}{\theta} \right) p dX_2$$

Now $dU > 0$ requires that $dX_2 \gtrless 0$ as $\theta \gtrless 1$. In other words, increase the output of X_2 when $\theta > 1$ and decrease the output of X_2 when $\theta < 1$. The output of X_2 can be increased or decreased by a suitable production tax-cum-subsidy policy. When $\theta > 1$ (<1) sector 2 suffers

Figure 8.2a

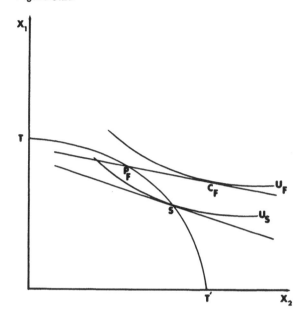

Figure 8.2b

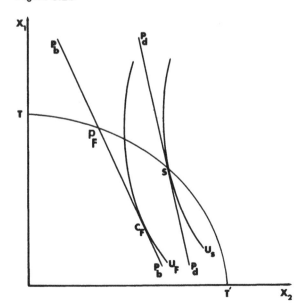

Figure 8.3a

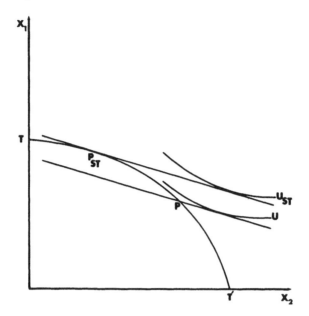

Figure 8.3b

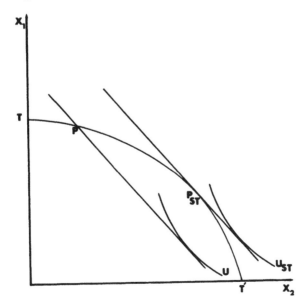

(benefits) from an external diseconomy (economy) from sector 1, hence in equilibrium output of X_2 is less (greater) than the optimal. Therefore increase (decrease) output of X_2 when $\theta > 1$ ($\theta < 1$). In fact a suitable production tax-cum-subsidy policy will take the economy to an optimal position as illustrated in Figures 8.3a and 8.3b. These figures are self-explanatory. Note that a tariff is not the optimal policy in this case. This is because in order to improve welfare we have only to alter production (as is obvious from equation (8.7)). A tariff affects both consumption and production as shown in Chapter 3, and hence it upsets the relation between the domestic rate of substitution and the foreign rate of transformation.

Theorem 8.1: In the presence of a Meade-type production externality free trade is not the optimal policy. The optimal policy is a production tax-cum-subsidy policy.

8.4 Externalities, Terms of Trade and Welfare

It is now appropriate to examine the proposition that for a small country a deterioration (improvement) in the terms of trade lowers (raises) welfare, when the economy is characterised by the presence of an externality.

By following the procedure used in Chapter 3, the following expression has been derived which shows the relationship between terms of trade and welfare:

$$\frac{1}{U_1} \frac{dU}{dp} = \left(\frac{\theta - 1}{\theta}\right) p \frac{dX_2}{dp} - M_2 \tag{8.8}$$

The second term in (8.8) is always negative. However, the sign of the first term depends on θ. In the presence of an externality $\theta \gtrless 1$. Suppose $\theta > 1$, this implies that the first term in equation (8.8) is positive, while the second term is negative. Hence the sign of $(1/U_1)(dU/dp)$ is ambiguous. It should be pointed out here that in the factor price differential case the breakdown of the standard proposition regarding terms of trade and welfare depends on two terms, $(1 - \beta)$ and dX_2/dp. In Chapter 2, we showed that dX_2/dp could be negative in the presence of a factor price differential. This perverse price output response can also lead to the breakdown of the normal relationship between terms of trade and welfare. In the externality case the price output response is normal, and hence the breakdown of the normal result arises due to the presence of θ, which reflects the direction of the externality.

Theorem 8.2: In the presence of a Meade-type production externality the proposition that for a small country a deterioration (improvement) in the terms of trade lowers (raises) welfare is false.

A better understanding of theorem 8.2 can be obtained with the help of a diagram. In Figure 8.4, TT′ represents the normal production possibility locus. At the original terms of trade given by the slope of P_0P_0 production equilibrium occurs at E and consumption equilibrium at C_0. The welfare level is indicated by U_0. Let the terms of trade deteriorate, which is indicated by the slope of the line P_dP_d. This price change causes production to occur at E′, consumption to occur at C_d. The welfare level is indicated by U_d. It is obvious that $U_d > U_0$, and hence welfare has risen as a consequence of the deterioration in the

Figure 8.4

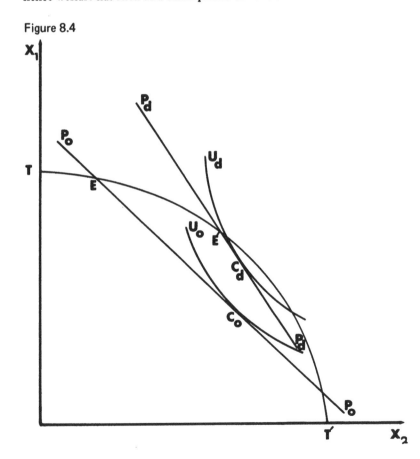

terms of trade. The welfare gain occurs because a deterioration in the terms of trade causes an increase in the output of the commodity which is socially more desirable and was originally being produced at the suboptimal level due to the externality. The deterioration in the terms of trade reduces the production loss imposed by the presence of an externality. If this gain is greater than the consumption loss due to the adverse movement in the terms of trade, then the deterioration in the terms of trade results in an improvement in welfare as illustrated in Figure 8.4.

8.5 Externalities and Rybczynski Theorem

In the Heckscher–Ohlin two-commodity, two-factor model, the Rybczynski theorem states that in an incompletely specialised economy, if the supply of one of the two primary factors of production is increased, at constant terms of trade, then the output of the commodity intensive in that factor will increase while that of the other commodity will decline absolutely. We shall now show that the Rybczynski theorem is affected by the presence of externalities and it does not predict correctly the direction of the output response of *one* of the commodities.

By differentiating equations (8.3) and (8.4) with respect to K, assuming all prices to be constant, we obtain:

$$\frac{dX_1}{dK} = f_1 \frac{dL_1}{dK} \tag{8.9}$$

$$\frac{dX_2}{dK} = f_2 \frac{dL_2}{dK} + L_2 g' f_1 \frac{dL_1}{dK} - \frac{X_1}{L_2} g' \frac{dL_2}{dK} \tag{8.10}$$

where

$$g' = \frac{\partial f_2}{\partial \left(\frac{X_1}{L_2} \right)}$$

and g' indicates the impact of the externality factor. The value of $g' > 0$ implies that sector 1 creates an external economy for sector 2 and $g' < 0$ indicates that sector 1 creates an external diseconomy for sector 2.

The solution for dL_i/dK ($i = 1, 2$) can be obtained from the factor endowment conditions. After obtaining these solutions and substitution in equations (8.9) and (8.10), we obtain:

$$\frac{dX_1}{dK} = \frac{f_1}{(k_1 - k_2)} \tag{8.11}$$

$$\frac{dX_2}{dK} = -\frac{f_2}{(k_1 - k_2)} + \frac{g'f_1}{L_2(k_1 - k_2)} \tag{8.12}$$

On the basis of equations (8.11) and (8.12) the signs of dX_i/dK ($i = 1, 2$) can be determined. Let us assume that $k_1 > k_2$. In this case the Rybczynski theorem predicts that $dX_1/dK > 0$ and $dX_2/dK < 0$, i.e. the capital-intensive sector expands and the labour-intensive sector contracts as a result of capital accumulation. This prediction of Rybczynski theorem may not hold in the presence of an externality.

We shall now show that in the presence of an externality the output of the labour-intensive sector may expand as a result of capital accumulation. Let us suppose that $g' > 0$, the case of an external economy. If $k_1 > k_2$, then only the first term in equation (8.12) is negative and the other term is positive. If the following inequality is satisfied, then the output of X_2, the labour-intensive sector, will rise as a consequence of capital accumulation:

$$\frac{-f_2}{(k_1 - k_2)} + \frac{g'f_1}{L_2(k_1 - k_2)} > 0 \tag{8.13}$$

Thus, if equation (8.13) is satisfied $dX_2/dK > 0$, even though $k_1 > k_2$ – a result that fails to satisfy the Rybczynski theorem. This happens because the output of sector 2 not only depends on the capital and labour inputs but also on the output of sector 1. Output of sector 1 rises as a consequence of capital accumulation (given our assumption that $k_1 > k_2$). This increase in the output of sector 1 exerts a favourable influence on the output of sector 2 due to the presence of an external economy, and at constant prices it may outweigh the loss in output arising from the movement of factors from sector 2 to sector 1. Hence, the failure of Rybczynski theorem in predicting the output of one of the sectors.

This result is presented diagrammatically in Figure 8.5, where TT is the pre-growth production possibility locus and $T'T'$ the post-growth production possibility locus. Production in the pre-growth situation occurs at point P_0 and in the post-growth situation at P_g. It is obvious from the diagram that at P_g the output of both sectors is more than the output of sectors 1 and 2 at the pre-growth equilibrium point P_0.

Theorem 8.3: In the presence of a Meade-type production externality the Rybczynski theorem does not hold.

Figure 8.5

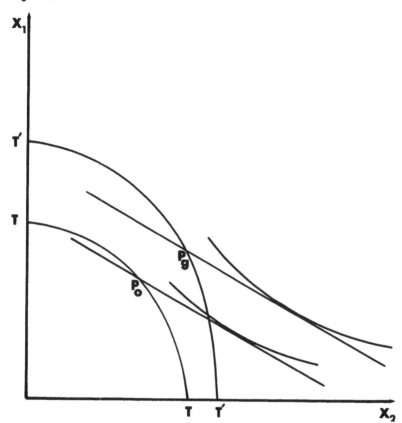

Theorem 8.3 is important for evaluating the impact of economic expansion on the terms of trade.

8.6 Technical Progress and Output Levels

In this subsection, we present a result (without proof) regarding the consequences of Hicks-neutral technical progress for output levels. Technical progress in sector 1 in the presence of a Meade-type production externality can be introduced in the same manner as in Chapter 4. In the first best framework Hicks-neutral technical progress in sector 1 results in an absolute increase in the output of sector 1 and an absolute decline in the output of sector 2. This need not be so in the presence of an externality. Suppose the output of sector 2 is affected by the presence of an external economy from sector 1 and that technical progress occurs in sector 1 leading to an expansion in its output. This increase in the output of sector 1 has a favourable impact on the output of sector 2 due to the presence of an externality. The favourable impact could be so large that it may outweigh the negative impact of technical progress in sector 1 on the output of sector 2, leading to an expansion of sector 2. This result can be easily proved with the help of calculus but this is not essential since the logic is intuitively obvious. It should be pointed out here that in the presence of an externality the output of the progressive industry cannot fall. Such a result can occur in the framework of factor price differentials. However, both outputs may rise as a consequence of technical progress in the framework of factor price differentials as well as in the case of a production externality.

8.7 Externalities and Immiserising Growth

In this section we examine the impact of capital accumulation on welfare. The need for examining the impact of other types of economic expansion is absent in the present context because their analysis in the externality framework is analytically similar to the case of factor accumulation.

By following the procedure used in Chapter 4 regarding the impact of factor accumulation on welfare, we obtain the following solution in the externality framework:

$$\frac{1}{U_1} \frac{dU}{dK} = r + g' \frac{f_1(1 + L_1)}{(k_1 - k_2)} \tag{8.14}$$

On the basis of equation (8.14) the following theorem can be established.

Theorem 8.4: For any physical-factor intensity ranking (excluding equal factor intensity) of industries 1 and 2 ($k_1 \gtrless k_2$) there exists an externality that will cause 'immiserising growth' as a result of capital accumulation at constant prices.

A proof of theorem 8.4 follows. Let us suppose $k_1 > k_2$. Now we know that $r > 0$. If $k_1 > k_2$ and $g' < 0$ then the second term in equation (8.14) is negative. Hence for $k_1 > k_2$ 'immiserising growth' will occur if the following inequality is satisfied:

$$r + g' \frac{f_1(1 + L_1)}{(k_1 - k_2)} < 0 \quad \left(\begin{matrix} k_1 > k_2 \\ g' < 0 \end{matrix} \right)$$

Suppose instead that $k_2 > k_1$. Again r is positive. Suppose further that

Figure 8.6

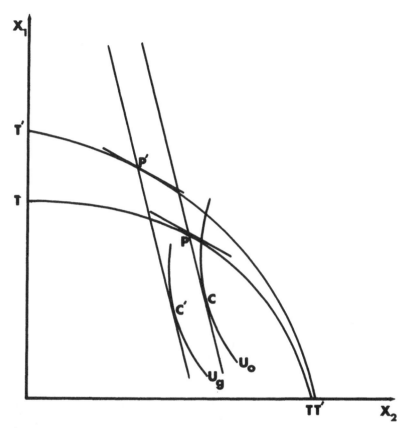

g' > 0, then given $k_2 > k_1$, it follows that the second term is negative. It follows immediately that 'immiserising growth' will occur if the following inequality is satisfied:

$$r + g' \frac{f_1(1 + L_1)}{(k_1 - k_2)} < 0 \quad \begin{pmatrix} k_2 > k_1 \\ g' > 0 \end{pmatrix}$$

Thus we have shown that for any physical ranking of industries (excluding equality) 1 and 2 ($k_1 \gtrless k_2$) there exists an externality that will cause 'immiserising growth' at constant prices.

The intuitive appeal of the theorem can be best brought out with the help of a diagram. We present a case of 'immiserising growth' in the presence of externalities. In Figure 8.6, let TT and T'T' be the pre-growth and post-growth transformation locuses and P and C represent the pre-growth production and consumption points while P' and C' represent the post-growth production and consumption points. Point C is welfare-wise superior to C' — hence 'immiserising growth'. The basic cause of 'immiserising growth' in this case is an over-expansion of industry 1 and excessive contraction of industry 2 due to external diseconomies created by industry 1.

The result contained in theorem 8.4 should be distinguished from theorems of 'immiserising growth' that arise in the factor price differential case. In the latter case 'immiserising growth' basically arises due to movement of labour from a high-productivity sector to a low-productivity sector as a result of economic expansion. Such a movement obviously causes a loss in welfare. In the externality case 'immiserising growth' arises due to over-expansion or excessive contraction of sectors from the social point of view due to the presence of external economy or diseconomy.

Results similar to theorem 8.4 can be obtained for technical progress and expansion of the labour supply. This has not been attempted because such an analysis does not add anything new to one's understanding of the working of the model in the presence of an externality.

8.8 Economic Expansion and the Terms of Trade

Finally, we present one result relating to the impact of economic expansion on the terms of trade. As already stated economic expansion can occur either due to technical progress and/or factor accumulation. We shall confine ourselves to factor accumulation — specifically to capital accumulation. This is done in order to highlight the difference in results relating to the impact of economic expansion on terms of trade in the factor price differential case, as opposed to the externality case.

By following the procedure outlined in Chapter 5 to obtain the expression for the impact of capital accumulation on terms of trade, we derive the following expression:

$$\frac{dp}{dK} = \frac{[m_h(1-\theta)-1]\frac{\partial X_2}{\partial K}}{[\epsilon_f + \epsilon_h - 1]M_2} \tag{8.15}$$

Given stability conditions, the denominator of equation (8.15) is positive. So the sign of dp/dK depends on the numerator. Assume that both goods are non-inferior in consumption which implies that $0 < m_h < 1$, hence, irrespective of the value of θ (i.e. $\theta \gtrless 1$), the bracketed term in the numerator is always negative. Hence, the sign of dp/dK is always opposite to the sign of $\partial X_2/\partial K$.

Let us further suppose that $k_1 > k_2$. In the standard case this assumption implies that $\partial X_2/\partial K < 0$. However, given the presence of an externality, the sign of $\partial X_2/\partial K$ is ambiguous, therefore the sign of dp/dK is ambiguous. Suppose $\partial X_2/\partial K > 0$, then the terms of trade move in favour of the expanding country, despite the fact that capital accumulation is biased in favour of the exporting industry.[6] In the case of a factor price differential this result cannot occur as a consequence of factor accumulation because in that case the Rybczynski theorem is valid. It is the invalidity of the Rybczynski theorem in the externality case that gives rise to this non-standard result regarding expansion and terms of trade. Output movements due to technical progress are ambiguous in the factor price differential case and these non-standard movements may lead to non-normal response of the terms of trade to technical progress (as shown in Chapter 5).

8.9 Summary

The consequences of a Meade-type pure production externality have been examined for several propositions in the pure theory of international trade. The following results have emerged from our investigation:

(1) Free trade cannot be uniquely ranked *vis-à-vis* no trade in the presence of Meade-type externality.

(2) *Laissez-faire* is not the optimal policy, when the economy is characterised by an externality. A production tax-cum-subsidy policy is the optimal policy.

(3) A deterioration (improvement) in the terms of trade may raise (lower) welfare in the presence of an externality.

(4) The Rybczynski theorem does not hold in the presence of an externality.

(5) For any physical-factor intensity ranking of industries excluding equality, there exists an externality that will cause 'immiserising growth'.

(6) The breakdown of the Rybczynski theorem also results in a breakdown of the traditional result on economic expansion and terms of trade, namely export-biased growth results in a deterioration of the

terms of trade.

Notes

1. Some of the consequences of this type of externality have been discussed by several trade theorists. See, for example, Bhagwati and Ramaswami (1), Haberler (5), Johnson (6) and Kemp (7).
2. The classic economic example of this type of externality is provided by Meade (18), (19). The Meade example relates to the case in which the bees feed on the nectar in the apple blossom. An externality arises because the apple farmer cannot arrange to charge the bee-keeper for the nectar sucked by the bees out of the apple blossom. Obviously, in this case the private value of apple production falls below its social value.
3. A rigorous proof of this result is available in Kemp (7). There also exist other types of production externalities that have an impact on the shape of the production possibility curve. In fact there exist some externalities that can lead to non-convexity of the production possibility set; see, for example, Baumol and Bradford (17), Kemp (7) and Starett (20).
4. We had remarked in footnote 3 that there exist externalities which result in a change in the shape of the transformation locus. For instance, detrimental externalities of the type considered by Baumol and Bradford (17) result in the shrinkage of the transformation locus. In extreme cases the locus becomes convex to the origin. This type of shrinkage should be distinguished from that which occurs in the case of factor price differential. The latter type of shrinkage is in principle removable by policy measures while the former type is not.
5. This standard result has already been discussed in Chapter 3 and its explanation need not be repeated again.
6. This result can be presented diagrammatically in the same manner as the case of the impact of economic expansion on terms of trade when the economy is characterised by a factor price differential. See Chapter 5.

References

Free Trade versus No Trade With and Without Meade-Type Pure Production Externality and Optimal Policy

(1) Bhagwati, J. N. and Ramaswami, V. K. 1963. Domestic Distortions, Tariffs and the Theory of Optimum Subsidy. *Journal of Political Economy*, Vol. 71 (February), 44–50.
(2) Bhagwati, J. N. 1968. The Gains from Trade Once Again. *Oxford Economic Papers*, Vol. 2 (July).
(3) Bhagwati, J. N., and Ramaswami, V. K. 1969. Domestic Distortions, Tariffs and the Theory of Optimum Subsidy: Some Further Results. *Journal of Political Economy*, Vol. 77 (September), 1005–10.
(4) Bhagwati, J. N. 1971. The Generalized Theory of Distortions and Welfare. In J. N. Bhagwati *et al.* (eds.), *Trade, Balance of Payments and Growth*. Papers in International Economics in Honour of Charles P. Kindleberger. Amsterdam: North Holland.
(5) Haberler, G. 1950. Some Problems in the Pure Theory of International Trade. *Economic Journal*, Vol. 60 (June), 223–40.
(6) Johnson, H. G. 1965. Optimal Trade Intervention in the Presence of Domestic Distortions. In R. E. Caves *et al.* (ed.), *Money, Trade and Growth*. Essays in

Honour of G. Haberler. Chicago: Rand-McNally.

(7) Kemp, M. C. 1969. *The Pure Theory of International Trade and Investment.* Englewood Cliffs, New Jersey: Prentice-Hall.

(8) Kemp, M. C. 1962. The Gain from International Trade. *Economic Journal,* Vol. 72 (December), 803–19.

(9) Kemp, M. C., and Negishi, T. 1969. Domestic Distortions, Tariffs and the Theory of Optimum Subsidy. *Journal of Political Economy,* Vol. 77 (November), 1011–13.

(10) Samuelson, P. A. 1939. The Gains from International Trade. *Canadian Journal of Economics and Political Science,* Vol. 5 (May), 195–205.

(11) Samuelson, P. A. 1962. The Gains from International Trade Once Again. *Economic Journal,* Vol. 62 (December), 820–9.

On Terms of Trade and Welfare

(12) Krueger, A. O., and Sonnenschein, H. 1967. The Terms of Trade, the Gains from Trade and Price Divergence. *International Economic Review,* Vol. 8 (February), 121–7.

On Rybczynski Theorem and Immiserising Growth in the Externalities Framework

(13) Hazari, B. R., and Sgro, P. M. 1974. Externalities, Rybczynski Theorem: And a Contrast between Immiserizing (Normal) Growth Theorems in the Traded and Non-Traded Goods Framework. *Indian Economic Journal,* Vol. 22 (October), 1–10.

(14) Rybczynski, T. M. 1955. Factor Endowments and Relative Commodity Prices. *Economica,* Vol. 22 (November), 336–41.

On Economic Expansion and Terms of Trade

(15) Findlay, R., and Grubert, H. 1959. Factor Intensity, Technological Progress and the Terms of Trade. *Oxford Economic Papers,* new series, Vol. 2 (February), 111–21.

(16) Hicks, J. R. 1953. An Inaugural Lecture: The Long-Run Dollar Problem. *Oxford Economic Papers,* Vol. 5 (June), 117–35.

On Externalities

(17) Baumol, W., and Bradford, D. 1972. Detrimental Externalities and Non-Convexity of the Production Set. *Economica,* Vol. 39 (May), 160–76.

(18) Meade, J. E. 1952. External Economies and Diseconomies in a Competitive Situation. *Economic Journal,* Vol. 62 (March), 54–67.

(19) Meade, J. E. 1973. *The Theory of Economic Externalities.* Geneva: Institut des Hautes Etudes Internationales.

(20) Starrett, D. A. 1972. Fundamental Nonconvexities in the Theory of Externalities. *Journal of Economic Theory,* Vol. 4 (April), 80–99.

9 MONOPOLY AND SOME PROPOSITIONS IN THE PURE THEORY OF TRADE

In the preceding chapter we considered one specific type of product market imperfection – the case of a pure production externality of the Meade variety. In this chapter we shall analyse the consequences of yet another type of product market imperfection, namely the presence of monopoly.[1] The assumption of perfect product markets is relaxed and instead it is assumed that either one or both industries are characterised by monopoly. Monopoly represents the polar opposite of the assumption of perfect competition. There are several market forms that lie between perfect competition and monopoly, for instance, duopoly and oligopoly. The real world is characterised probably more by these intermediate market forms than by the extreme cases of perfect competition and monopoly. However, in studying market imperfections, monopoly provides us with a case that is not as difficult to handle as, say, oligopoly. Moreover, an analysis of monopoly provides some insight into the workings of imperfect markets.

Although the ultimate concern of the present chapter is with the impact of monopoly on some propositions in the pure theory of trade, it is important to discuss the autarky equilibrium initially. This is necessitated by the difficulties associated with the existence of an equilibrium, when an economy is characterised by monopoly. In the monopoly case a meaningful solution, from the economist's point of view, may not exist for all demand elasticities. After all, from elementary micro theory we know that a monopolist never produces at a point where the price elasticity of demand is less than unity. After characterising the autarky equilibrium, we discuss the ranking of free trade *vis-à-vis* no trade and finally the implications of monopoly for the Lerner symmetry theorem.[2]

9.1 The Model With Monopoly

Before characterising the autarky equilibrium under monopoly, it is necessary to make some changes in the equations of the model presented in Chapter 1. The equations that need change relate to payment to factors, capital and labour. From micro theory, it is known that the real reward of each factor in monopoly equals marginal revenue product rather than the value of marginal product. Marginal revenue in the ith sector is defined as:

$$M.R._i = p_i\left(1 - \frac{1}{\eta_i}\right) \quad i = 1, 2$$

where η_i is the price elasticity of demand for the ith product. It follows that:

$$w = \left(1 - \frac{1}{\eta_1}\right)[f_1 - k_1 f_1'] = p\left[1 - \frac{1}{\eta_2}\right][f_2 - k_2 f_2'] \tag{9.1}$$

$$r = \left(1 - \frac{1}{\eta_1}\right)f_1' = p\left(1 - \frac{1}{\eta_2}\right)f_2' \tag{9.2}$$

Given the assumption that the production functions are homogeneous of degree one it follows from Euler's theorem that the output in each sector must equal the sum of returns to the two factors of production capital and labour. However, in monopoly the factors of production are paid the marginal revenue product (not value of marginal product), and hence the sum of returns to factors cannot equal the value of output. The difference total revenue minus total costs represents excess profits, i.e.

$$E_{\pi_1} = \frac{X_1 - (rK_1 - wL_1)}{X_1} = \frac{1}{\eta_1} \tag{9.3}$$

$$E_{\pi_2} = \frac{pX_2 - p(rK_2 - wL_2)}{X_2} = \frac{p}{\eta_2} \tag{9.4}$$

where $E_{\pi i}$ ($i = 1, 2$) denotes excess profits. It is important to emphasise that there is no conflict between the assumption of constant returns to scale and monopoly. The excess of revenue over factor costs accrues to the entrepreneurs as abnormal profit. In the perfectly competitive case $\eta_i = \infty$, which implies that abnormal or excess profits equal zero. The positivity of excess profits ($E_{\pi i} > 0$, $i = 1, 2$) in monopoly immediately brings up the problem of determining demand elasticities (η_i, $i = 1, 2$). The demand elasticities in the present chapter are obtained from a social utility function which is assumed to be of the constant elasticity of substitution type.[3]

If we assume that the economy is closed then $D_i = X_i$ and the constant elasticity of substitution utility function takes the following form:

$$U = U(D_1, D_2) = (aX_1^{-\gamma} + bX_2^{-\gamma})^{-1/\gamma}$$

a, b and γ are parameters. While a and b are assumed to be positive, γ is assumed to take on values in the following interval, $-1 < \gamma < \infty, \gamma \neq 0$. Let $\sigma_D = 1/1 + \gamma$, where σ_D denotes the elasticity of substitution in consumption.[4] In order to simplify the analysis, it is assumed that $a/b = 1$. The demand functions associated with the constant elasticity of substitution utility function are:[5]

$$X_1 = \frac{Y}{p_1(1 + p^{\gamma\sigma}D)}, \quad X_2 = \frac{Y}{p_2(1 + p^{-\gamma\sigma}D)}$$

$$\therefore \frac{X_1}{X_2} = \frac{p(1 + p^{-\gamma\sigma}D)}{(1 + p^{\gamma\sigma}D)} = p^{\sigma}D, \quad \text{where} \quad \left(p = \frac{p_2}{p_1}\right) \tag{9.5}$$

From these demand functions the elasticities of demand η_1 and η_2 are:

$$\eta_1 = \frac{1 + \sigma_D p^{\gamma\sigma}D}{1 + p^{\gamma\sigma}D} \tag{9.6}$$

$$\eta_2 = \frac{1 + \sigma_D p^{-\gamma\sigma}D}{1 + p^{-\gamma\sigma}D} \tag{9.7}$$

Two observations need to be made regarding η_1 and η_2. First, both the elasticities depend solely on the ratio of prices and not on income. This is due to the homotheticity of the utility function. Second, it is obvious from the expressions for η_1 and η_2 that $\eta_i \gtreqless 1$ as $\sigma_D \gtreqless 1$.

We have completed the specification of the model with monopoly and our task now is to derive some results.

9.2 The Autarky Equilibrium

In order to demonstrate the problems associated with the existence of an equilibrium with monopoly in the two-sector model, we begin with a brief recapitulation of the perfectly competitive case. In the perfectly competitive framework, given the production functions and the endowment conditions, the concave to the origin production possibility curve is obtained.[6] An equilibrium is attained at the point where the social indifference curve is tangential to the transformation locus. At such a point consumers maximise utility, producers maximise profits and demand equals supply. In arriving at the equilibrium position in the competitive case the consumers and producers act independently, that is consumers maximise utility subject to a budget constraint and producers maximise profits subject to given technology and prices. From

Figure 9.1

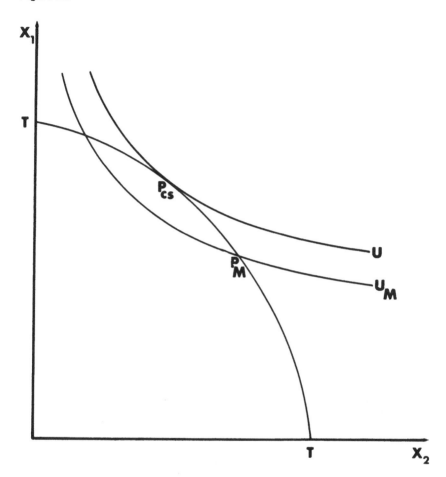

these maximisation procedures the demand and supply functions are generated. An equilibrium is established at a point where all markets are cleared, that is, product and factor markets. This is represented by point P_{cs} in Figure 9.1.

Suppose we assume that both X_1 and X_2 are produced by monopolies. While the consumers still maximise utility subject to a budget constraint independently of the producers, the monopolist cannot maximise profits without knowledge of the demand conditions. The monopolists require data on demand for the product in order to make profit-maximising price–output decision. To bring this point out clearly, we need a characterisation of the slope of the production possibility curve which is nothing other than the ratio of marginal costs. Before obtaining this expression it should be observed that in the monopoly case the economy operates on the first best locus. The production possibility curve does not shrink because the marginal rates of factor substitution are identical between the two sectors. The relation between the slope of the production possibility curve and the commodity price ratio can be derived by following the procedure used in Chapter 1. It follows:

$$\frac{M.C_{x_2}}{M.C_{x_1}} = \frac{dX_1}{dX_2} = -p \left[\frac{1 - \frac{1}{\eta_2}}{1 - \frac{1}{\eta_1}} \right] = -p\delta \tag{9.8}$$

where MC_{xi} denotes the marginal cost in sector i (i = 1, 2). From equation (9.8) several conclusions follow. First, if $\eta_1 = \eta_2$, then monopoly will give rise to the same production position as the perfectly competitive case, because $dX_1/dX_2 = -p$. However, this is only one of an infinite number of solutions that exist. Second, it is obvious from equation (9.8) that if the demand elasticities are less (η_i, i = 1, 2) than unity, then (9.8) implies that marginal costs are negative. Since negative marginal costs make no economic sense the value of demand elasticities must be restricted in order to derive a meaningful equilibrium. To obtain a meaningful economic solution, we require that both the elasticities be greater than unity. Thus, a necessary condition for the monopoly equilibrium to exist is that both the price elasticities of demand η_1 and η_2 be greater than one. This assumption is the same as $\sigma_D > 1$.

Equation (9.8) also makes it clear why we must be concerned with the existence of an equilibrium in the monopoly case. Suppose we specify a price ratio P_c for the consumers. Given the demand functions generated from the constant elasticity of substitution utility function, as soon as we specify P_c we know the unique ratio in which commodities X_1 and X_2 will be consumed. Since the ratio in which they are consumed is known, we also know the demand elasticities. Given the demand elasticities, from the marginal productivity conditions, the producer's price ratio P_P will be determined. The existence problem is whether the producer's price ratio P_P will equal the consumer's price ratio P_c.[8] The existence of monopoly equilibrium may be proved by first establishing a relation between consumer's price ratio P_c and the wage–rental ratio. This can be done with the help of equation (9.5). The left-hand side on differentiation shows changes in X_1 and X_2 and the right-hand side in P_c. Changes in X_1 and X_2 are obviously related to the wage–rental ratio, therefore P_c is also related to the wage–rental ratio. A similar relationship is established between the producer's price ratio P_P and the wage–rental ratio. It is then shown that these two relationships are opposite in sign (two curves are opposite in slope) and intersect with each other at a unique point, which gives the equilibrium.

The autarky equilibrium in the monopoly case is diagrammatically presented in Figure 9.1. We shall assume that $\eta_1 \neq \eta_2$. In the perfectly competitive case production and consumption equilibrium occurs at P_{cs}. The welfare level associated with this point is indicated by U. The monopoly equilibrium occurs at the consumption-production point P_M. Obviously, P_M is located on a lower indifference curve than U, and hence monopoly results in a loss in welfare.

One other point that needs emphasis is that in terms of consequences the Meade-type pure production externality and monopoly both result in the same inequality, namely, DRS $\neq$ DRT. However, the economic logic behind the occurrence of the inequality is different.

9.3 Monopoly and the Gains from Trade

In this section, we wish to examine the welfare consequences of opening our closed model to trade.

The opening of the model immediately raises the question of whether domestic monopolies can survive foreign competition or not. If it is assumed that the country is small and cannot influence world prices then it immediately follows that in allowing trade to occur the monopolies disappear. Hence, in this case free trade turns out to be not only better than autarky but also the optimal commercial policy. Trade in this case results in three types of gain: the consumption gain, the production gain and the gain from the removal of a domestic distortion. This is illustrated in Figure 9.2. The figure is self-explanatory.[9]

Let us now consider a different scenario. Suppose there are two countries, home and foreign, and industries in both countries are assumed to be monopolies. If trade is allowed in this model, then the situation immediately becomes one of duopoly – two firms producing X_1 and two firms producing X_2. A way out of this is to assume that the two firms producing each of the two goods are owned and controlled by the same company, that is, two companies each with a home firm and a foreign subsidiary.[10]

In the section on autarky equilibrium we commented on the

Figure 9.2

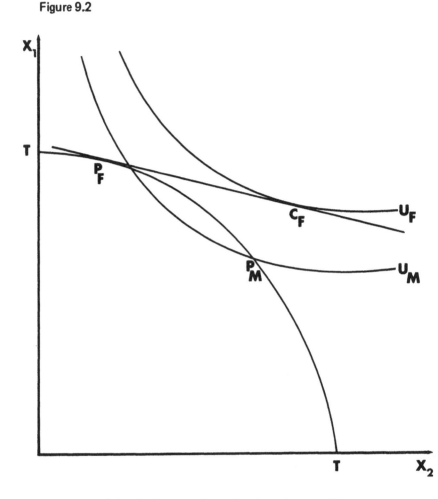

importance of the elasticity condition for the existence of the equilibrium. When the model is open, commodities are sold both in the home and foreign market. The question arises as to what elasticities are relevant when sales occur both in the domestic as well as foreign markets? This question can be resolved without much difficulty. Suppose both countries have identical constant elasticity of substitution utility functions. It follows from this assumption that at identical prices the demand elasticities in the two countries are the same. This is so because with identical prices both the countries must consume commodities in an identical ratio. In the open model the relevant

Figure 9.3a

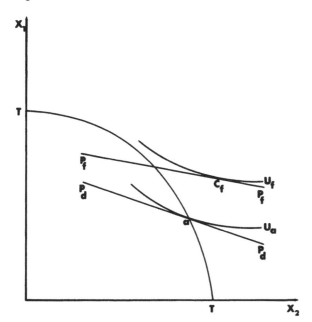

Figure 9.3b

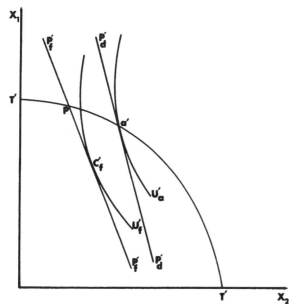

elasticity is the one associated with the world consumption of commodities rather than the elasticity at the point of local production. This elasticity is not relevant because in an open model production and consumption points are not identical. It is now appropriate to examine the welfare ranking of free trade *vis-à-vis* no trade.

In Figures 9.3a and 9.3b we present two cases. In one case free trade is welfare-wise better than no trade, whilst in the other, autarky is better than free trade. In both cases free trade is a suboptimal policy. We shall discuss only the latter case in detail. $T'T'$ in Figure 9.3b is the production possibility locus. Let us suppose that $\eta_1 > \eta_2$. It follows from equation (9.8) that δ in this case is less than one. Hence, at the point of autarky equilibrium a', the domestic rate of transformation is less than the domestic price ratio given by the slope of line $P'_d P'_d$. Suppose the free-trade price ratio is given by the slope of $P'_f P'_f$. The price ratio has moved in favour of commodity X_1. Hence, output of X_1 rises and that of X_2 falls. Output now moves to point P and consumption to point C'_f. The country exports X_1 and imports X_2. The welfare is indicated by U'_f. But $U'_f < U'_a$, therefore free trade in terms of welfare is worse than no trade. The welfare-wise superiority of free trade over no trade is shown in Figure 9.3a. Hence it follows that *free trade cannot be uniquely ranked vis-à-vis no trade in the presence of monopoly.*

9.4 Lerner Symmetry Theorem and Monopoly

In 1936, Lerner proved the important theorem that in the standard model of trade, a tariff on the imported good at an *ad valorem* rate t_M is equivalent in its effect on real variable to an *ad valorem* tax of the same rate t_E on the exported commodity. In a recent paper Ray (9) demonstrated that the Lerner theorem did not hold in the presence of monopoly. We shall first present the Lerner symmetry theorem and then show its invalidity in the framework of monopoly.

Assume that there is no monopoly and the framework of analysis is characterised by first best assumptions. In this framework, if we impose a tax on exports t_E and a tax on imports t_M the following conditions on prices hold:

Import Tariff Situation	*Export Tax Situation*
p_1	$p_1^H = \dfrac{p_1}{(1 + t_E)}$
$p_2^H = (1 + t_M)p$	p_2

The relative price structure associated with the above situations will be:

Tariff

$$p_H = p(1 + t_M)$$

Tax

$$\frac{p_H}{(1 + t_E)} = p$$

where p_H denotes the domestic price ratio and p the international price ratio. If $t_E = t_M$ it immediately follows that the relative price structure is identical. Given that the supply functions are homogeneous of degree zero the outputs at the point of equilibrium must be the same. Now we only have to show that the demand generated for the two commodities is also identical. In contrast with the supply functions, demand depends on relative prices and real income. Hence, for the symmetry theorem to work, it must be shown that real income associated with the tariff situation is the same as the real income associated with the tax situation, in terms of domestic prices. The real income in the tariff situation in terms of domestic prices is given by:

$$Y_M = X_1 + p_H X_2 + t_M p_{M_2}$$

In the case of the export tax:

$$Y_E = X_1 + p_H X_2 + \frac{t_E}{1 + t_E} E_1$$

The terms $t_M p_{M_2}$ and $(t_E/1 + t_E)E_1$ represent the tariff and tax revenue respectively. These terms look different but in fact they are identical. The apparent difference is attributable to the choice of numeraire. Hence, after adjusting for the difference in absolute prices, $t_M p_{M_2} = (t_E E_1/1 + t_E)$. Therefore $Y_M = Y_E$. All this implies that under the two tax régimes production, consumption, imports and exports are identical.

The Lerner symmetry theorem is diagrammatically represented in Figure 9.4. The slope of the line $P_F P_F$ indicates the international price ratio. At this price ratio, free-trade production equilibrium occurs at P_0 and consumption equilibrium at C_F. Commodity X_1 is exported and X_2 imported. Given our restrictions on production functions and non-equality of factor intensities the production possibility curve TT is concave to the origin. This concavity in the absence of any factor price differentials implies a one-to-one correspondence between output supplies and the commodity price ratio. Hence, a tariff on imports of X_2 and a tax on exports of X_1, which give rise to the same price ratio, must generate the same production point. A tariff or an equivalent export tax moves the economy to point P_T in Figure 9.4. Consumption

Figure 9.4

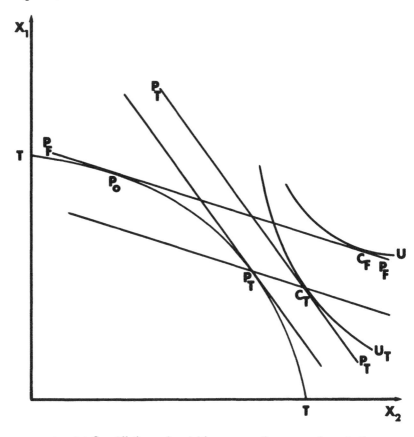

occurs at point C_T. All the real variables assume the same value whether we impose a tariff on imports or a tax on exports.

It is now appropriate to examine the Lerner symmetry theorem in the presence of monopoly. Without any loss in generality monopoly will from now on be assumed to be present in the importing sector only, hence:

$$w = p_1(f_1 - k_1 f_1') = p_2 \left(1 - \frac{1}{\eta_2}\right)(f_2 - k_2 f_2') \qquad (9.9)$$

$$r = p_1 f_1' = p_2 \left(1 - \frac{1}{\eta_2}\right)f_2' \qquad (9.10)$$

The Lerner symmetry theorem breaks down in the presence of

monopoly because factor prices in this framework are not homogeneous of degree one in output prices. Hence, it becomes important to distinguish relative prices from absolute prices. We demonstrate first rigorously the lack of homogeneity of degree one of factor prices (and later offer some intuitive comments).

Given the assumption of monopoly in the production of commodity X_2,

$$p = \frac{p_2\left(1 - \dfrac{1}{\eta_2}\right)}{p_1} \tag{9.11}$$

From (9.11) it follows:

$$\frac{dp}{dp_1} = -\frac{p}{p_1} \tag{9.12}$$

$$\frac{dp}{dp_2} = \frac{1}{p_1}\left(1 - \frac{1}{\eta_2} + \frac{p_2}{\eta_2}\frac{d\eta_2}{dp_2}\right) \tag{9.13}$$

By using equations (1.13), (1.15) and (9.11) to (9.13) it follows:

$$\frac{p_1}{w}\frac{dw}{dp_1} = -\frac{k_2}{\omega}\left[\frac{k_1 + \omega}{(k_1 - k_2)}\right] \tag{9.14}$$

$$\frac{p_2}{w}\frac{dw}{dp_2} = \left[\frac{1 + \dfrac{p_2}{\eta_2}\dfrac{d\eta_2}{dp_2}}{\eta_2 - 1}\right]\left[\frac{k_1}{w}\frac{\omega + k_2}{k_1 - k_2}\right] \tag{9.15}$$

From (9.14) and (9.15) it follows:

$$\frac{p_1}{w}\frac{dw}{dp_1} + \frac{p_2}{w}\frac{dw}{dp_2} = 1 - \left(\frac{\dfrac{p_2}{\eta_2}\dfrac{d\eta_2}{dp_2}}{(\eta_2 - 1)}\right)\left[\frac{k_1}{\omega}\frac{(\omega + k_2)}{(k_2 - k_1)}\right] \tag{9.16}$$

Similarly, it can be shown that:

$$\frac{p_1}{r}\frac{dr}{dp_1} + \frac{p_2}{r}\frac{dr}{dp_2} = 1 + \frac{\omega + k_2}{(k_2 - k_1)}\left(\frac{\dfrac{p_2}{\eta_2}\dfrac{d\eta_2}{dp_2}}{(\eta_2 - 1)}\right) \tag{9.17}$$

Equations (9.16) and (9.17) show that factor prices are not homogeneous of degree one in output prices. It is important to explain the meaning of the above result. Suppose that both p_1 and p_2 are raised by 1 per cent. The relative price p_2/p_1 remains unaltered. The question here is what happens to factor prices? From (9.16) and (9.17) the changes in the wage are different from the change in the rental on capital. Equations (9.16) and (9.17) indicate that the percentage change in w and r will be one minus the second term on the right-hand side of (9.16) for w and one plus the second term on the right-hand side of (9.17) for r. Let us now suppose that a tariff is imposed on commodity 2, the imported commodity. Suppose further that the imposition of the tariff makes the production of X_2 less competitive. Then, $d\eta_2/dp_2$ will be negative and monopoly profits will rise by a decrease in the output of X_2. Suppose further that $k_2 > k_1$. It then follows that the right-hand side of (9.16) ((9.17)) will be greater (less) than one. Thus as long as $d\eta_2/dp_2 \neq 0$ the homogeneity conditions will not hold.

To show the invalidity of the Lerner symmetry theorem, we shall assume that $d\eta_2/dp_2 < 0$. This implies that an increase in p_1 and p_2 will be associated with a relative rise in w and a lower increase in r. The level of absolute prices is not identical when a tariff is imposed *vis-à-vis* a tax on exports. In the tariff situation the absolute price level is higher than in the export tax situation. It follows from (9.16) and (9.17) that ω, the wage–rental ratio, will be higher in the tariff situation in comparison with the tax situation. This implies that the output of X_1, the labour-intensive sector, could be greater than that which might be achieved with a tax on exportables. Hence, an import tariff and a tax under monopoly may have assymetrical output effects. Therefore, a tariff that is equivalent in rate to an export tax need not lead to the same production point.[11] If the production points are not identical then the Lerner symmetry theorem cannot hold.

The breakdown of the Lerner symmetry theorem in the presence of monopoly is shown in Figure 9.5. TT' is the normal production possibility locus. The free-trade production equilibrium at the international prices indicated by the slope of PP occurs at P_F. To avoid cluttering of the diagram the explicit representation of consumption equilibrium has been omitted. At point P_F, OX_2^F of X_2 is produced. Note that the output of X_2 is less than would have prevailed in the competitive situation. This is of course due to the presence of monopoly in the production of X_2. Now suppose we levy a tariff on X_2. The imposition of a tariff on X_2 has two effects: (a) it raises the relative domestic price of commodity 2 and (b) it lowers the relative world price of good 2. The former effect is indicated by the slope of P_dP_d and the latter by the slope of $P'P'$. The domestic output of X_2 falls from OX_2^F to OX_2^T. The degree of monopoly has obviously increased. If, as an alternative to a tariff, a tax on exportables is imposed such that it results in the same international and domestic

Figure 9.5

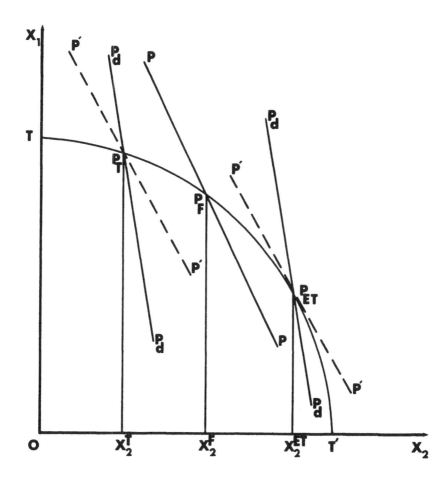

price ratio as the tariff, then output moves to point P_{ET}. Output of X_2 in this case rises from OX_2^T to OX_2^{ET}. The output points for the same *ad valorem* rate of tariff and export tax are not identical, and hence the Lerner symmetry theorem cannot hold in the case depicted in Figure 9.5.

9.5 Summary

In this chapter we have shown that the presence of monopoly leads to a non-unique ranking of free trade *vis-à-vis* no trade. We have also shown that the Lerner symmetry theorem does not hold in the presence of monopoly. Thus, the presence of monopoly has an impact on normative as well as positive propositions in trade theory. However, its impact is not as devastating of standard trade results as is the case of factor price differentials. In the presence of factor price differentials almost all the standard theorems of international trade do not hold. In the case of monopoly several trade theorems continue to be valid, for example the Heckscher–Ohlin theorem, factor price equalisation theorem and the Rybczynski, and its dual, the Stolper–Samuelson theorem.[12]

Notes

1. The implications of monopoly for the theory of international trade were first discussed in two important and pioneering papers by Batra (2) and Melvin and Warne (8).

2. Ray (9) in an important paper analysed the implications of monopoly for the Lerner symmetry theorem.

3. To simplify the problem of the existence of a solution in the monopoly case this type of utility function was first introduced in the literature by Melvin and Warne (8).

4. A more detailed treatment of this elasticity of substitution on the demand side is available in Batra (1) and Jones (6).

5. An explicit derivation of these demand functions is available in Batra (1) and Melvin and Warne (8). The standard technique of utility maximisation subject to a budget constraint is used for obtaining the demand functions.

6. See the discussion in Chapter 1 of the present book.

7. The distribution of income, however, will not be the same as in the competitive case, due to the presence of monopoly profits.

8. A formal proof of the existence is available in Batra (1) and Melvin and Warne (8).

9. The gain from the removal of domestic distortion can be seen more clearly in terms of a partial equilibrium diagram. This is done in Caves and Jones (4), pages 207–10.

10. An alternative assumption is that each firm acts as if it were a monopoly and treats its share of the world market as the total market for the commodity. These assumptions are not necessary in a more general model, for instance, in a model in which there is a non-traded good produced by a monopolist. This has recently been done by Cassing (3).

11. The ambiguity in the movement of monopoly output in relation with tariff is discussed in Finger (5).

12. The validity of these theorems in the monopoly framework is discussed in Batra (1) and Melvin and Warne (8). However, these results do not extend to the case where one good is assumed to be non-traded and others traded; see Cassing (3).

References

(1) Batra, R. N. 1973. *Studies in the Pure Theory of International Trade*. London: Macmillan.

(2) Batra, R. N. 1972. Monopoly Theory in General Equilibrium and the Two-Sector Model of Economic Growth. *Journal of Economic Theory*, Vol. 4 (June), 355–71.

(3) Cassing, J. 1977. International Trade in the Presence of Pure Monopoly in Non-Traded Goods Sector. *Economic Journal*, Vol. 87 (September), 523–31.

(4) Caves, R. E., and Jones, R. W. 1973. *World Trade and Payments: An Introduction*. Boston: Little, Brown.

(5) Finger, J. M. 1971. Protection and Domestic Output. *Journal of International Economics*, Vol. 1 (August), 345–51.

(6) Jones, R. W. 1965. The Structure of Simple General Equilibrium Models. *Journal of Political Economy*, Vol. 73 (December), 557–72.

(7) Lerner, A. P. 1936. The Symmetry Between Import and Export Taxes. *Economica*, Vol. 3 (August), 306–13.

(8) Melvin, J. R., and Warne, R. D. 1973. Monopoly and the Theory of International Trade. *Journal of International Economics*, Vol. 3 (May), 117–34.

(9) Ray, E. J. 1975. The Impact of Monopoly Pricing on the Lerner Symmetry Theorem. *Quarterly Journal of Economics*, Vol. 89 (November), 591–602.

Part Four

TARIFFS, ILLEGAL TRADE AND
IMMISERISING GROWTH

10 TARIFFS, SMUGGLING, WELFARE AND IMMISERISING GROWTH

This part of the book consists of only one chapter,[1] which is devoted to analysing some consequences of imposing a tariff in the small-country framework. Extraordinarily high tariffs exist in many developing countries. There are many reasons for the imposition of these tariffs[2] – economic and non-economic. For instance, tariffs may be imposed for collecting revenue; tariffs may be levied to curb non-essential consumption; tariffs may be used to attain a production goal.[3] However, for a small country facing fixed terms of trade the use of a tariff results in a distortion. This is so because for a small country free trade is the optimal policy. The imposition of the tariff results in inequality between the domestic rate of substitution in consumption which equals the domestic rate of transformation in production and the foreign rate of transformation (DRS = DRT ≠ FRT). Tariff distortion also generates interesting and perverse results. It is the purpose of this chapter to present some of these results.

Our focus of attention is on the welfare consequences of tariff-induced smuggling and the impact of economic expansion on welfare in the presence of a tariff without smuggling. This is the focus of attention because smuggling is a widely prevalent activity in many less-developed countries. It arises mainly as a tariff-induced phenomenon. Moreover, smuggling takes on *large proportions* in the developing countries due to the lax and corruptible enforcement of the law – hence the necessity of incorporating smuggling in the pure theory of international trade.[4] Since, in the presence of tariffs, economic expansion can result in 'immiserising growth', it is important to present some cases of the occurrence of this perverse result also.

We shall first discuss smuggling and then the implications of economic expansion on welfare in the presence of a tariff without smuggling.

10.1 The Model with Smuggling

We now wish to incorporate smuggling into the model presented in Chapter 1. Smuggling is introduced in the model with the help of a smuggling transformation curve.[5] This is so because smuggling is only another way of converting exportables into importables and vice versa.

This transformation (smuggling) curve will be assumed to be less favourable than the legal terms of trade.

We shall assume that there is perfect competition in smuggling.[6] The smuggling offer curve will be assumed to be characterised either by a constant rate of transformation or an increasing rate of transformation. Let $p_s = p_{2s}/p_{1s}$ denote the smugglers' price ratio. If it is assumed that there are constant costs in smuggling, then $p_s = \bar{p}_s$. In the case of increasing costs $p_s = g(E_s)/E_s$ where E_s represents smuggled exports. It is assumed that $g'(E_s) > 0$ and $g''(E_s) > 0$ so that p_s increases as E_s increases. Furthermore, $p_s < g'(E_s)$.

In order to introduce smuggling, we also need to modify the commodity balance equations. Equations (1.3) and (1.4) now become:

$$D_1 = X_1 - E_\varrho - E_s \tag{10.1}$$

$$D_2 = X_2 + M_\varrho + M_s \tag{10.2}$$

where E_ϱ denotes exports via the legal channel, E_s exports via the illegal channel, M_ϱ legal imports and M_s smuggled imports.

In the model with smuggling, we also need to distinguish three prices: p_d, the domestic price ratio, p_s, the smugglers' price ratio, and p_ϱ, the legal international price ratio. All the prices are defined in terms of good 1, the exportable commodity. We assume the country to be small, so that $p_\varrho = \bar{p}_\varrho$. For smuggling to occur a tariff is needed. Let t represent the rate of tariff, hence, $p = \bar{p}_\varrho(1 + t)$.

The balance of payments equation needs to be written in a way that it accommodates illegal trade. This equation takes the following form:

$$p_\varrho M_\varrho + p_s M_s = E_\varrho + E_s \tag{10.3}$$

The equation is self-explanatory.

The remainder of the equations in Chapter 1 are not affected by the introduction of illegal trade, and do not need to be modified. We are now in a position to analyse the impact of smuggling on welfare.

10.2 Impact of Smuggling on Welfare When Legal Trade is Eliminated by Smuggling

Our interest in this section of the work is to discuss the impact of smuggling on welfare, given the assumption that legal trade has been eliminated. The way the system works is the following. Assume that there is a tariff at the *ad valorem* rate t. The imposition of the tariff, given the small-country assumption, creates a difference between the international price ratio and the domestic price ratio. This divergence between the two price ratios creates an incentive for smuggling. Assume that as a consequence smuggling occurs and leads to the elimination of legal trade. This implies that the terms M_Q and E_Q become equal to zero. Only illegal trade remains in the model.

Given the assumption made earlier in this chapter of perfect competition, the elimination of legal trade implies that $p_s = p_d$. If we further assume constant costs then $p_s = \bar{p}_s$. So we have:

$$p_Q = \bar{p}_Q, \quad M_Q = 0, \quad E_Q = 0, \quad p_s = p_d, \quad p_s = \bar{p}_s$$

These conditions taken with the rest of the model determine the equilibrium. Our task is to compare the level of welfare associated with smuggling U_s and tariff U_t. Suppose that the smuggling price ratio coincides with the tariff-inclusive price ratio, i.e. $p_d = p_s = \bar{p}Q (1 + t)$. The welfare associated with the tariff equilibrium will be higher because smuggling occurs at inferior terms of trade compared with the tariff situation. Both the situations have the same production point, and hence welfare must be lower in the case where the terms of trade are unfavourable.

This result can easily be represented geometrically. In Figure 10.1, TT' is the production possibility locus. Free-trade production equilibrium occurs at P_F. The welfare associated with the free-trade position is indicated by U_F. A tariff is now imposed which takes production to P_t and consumption to C_t. The welfare level in the new situation is indicated by U_t. If the smugglers' price ratio coincides with the domestic price ratio, i.e. $p_s = p_d$, then in terms of diagram it implies that production with smuggling occurs at $P_s = P_t$. Consumption with smuggling occurs at C_s. The welfare level is indicated by U_s, but since $U_s < U_t$ smuggling becomes worse in welfare terms than the tariff equilibrium.

It is important to note here the way in which the costs of smuggling are introduced in the model. This is done in the same way as Samuelson introduced transport costs in the theory of international trade. Samuelson (9) states: 'that just as only a fraction of the ice exported reaches its destination as unmelted ice, so will a_x and a_y be the fractions of exports x and y that respectively reach the other country as imports'. Thus, the cost of smuggling in the present model is represented by the goods that perish in the process of being smuggled. This can happen, for instance, when goods are dumped to avoid detection. The critical point to note is that smuggling costs do not involve the use of any primary factors of production.[7]

It is now appropriate to discuss what happens to welfare when the price that smugglers offer changes from being equal to the tariff-

Figure 10.1

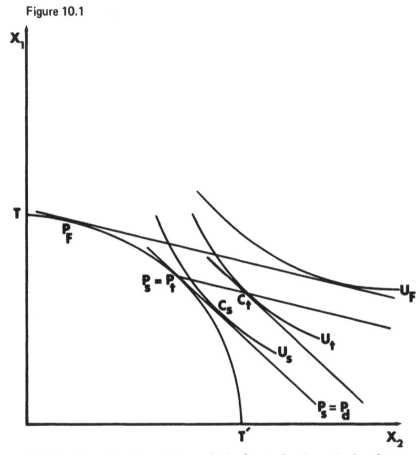

inclusive domestic price ratio towards the free-trade price ratio. In other words, what happens to welfare when $p_d = p_s$ falls below $\bar{p}_\varrho(1 + t)$. The result can be obtained by differentiating the utility function with respect to p_d and by utilising the technique used in earlier chapters for computing welfare changes. We obtain the following expression:

$$\frac{dU}{dp_d} = -U_1 M_s < 0 \qquad (10.4)$$

This expression shows that as p_d falls below the tariff-inclusive domestic price ratio $\bar{p}_\varrho(1 + t)$, the level of welfare associated with smuggling increases. Obviously, if p_d becomes less than $\bar{p}_\varrho$, the free-trade equilibrium is reached and $U_s > U_t$. This implies that there exists a point at which the level of welfare associated with smuggling just

Figure 10.2a

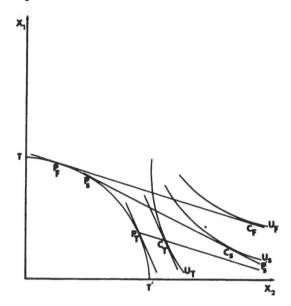

Figure 10.2b

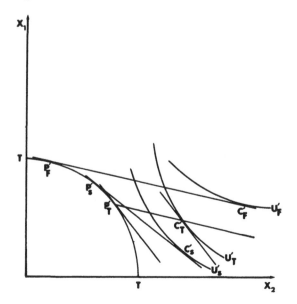

becomes equal to the level of welfare associated with the tariff equilibrium. Beyond this point, of course, $U_s > U_t$.

It should be observed here that if the tariff is prohibitive then the economy is characterised by an autarky equilibrium. The price ratio associated with this equilibrium is the same as the one at which the switch occurs between smuggling being a welfare-reducing to a welfare-increasing activity. Since only unilateral displacements are possible in this case, smuggling necessarily improves welfare. Thus, in the case of a prohibitive tariff smuggling in welfare terms is necessarily better than the tariff equilibrium.

In Figures 10.2a and 10.2b we illustrate the cases in which smuggling raises (lowers) welfare compared with the tariff position respectively. Let us consider Figure 10.2a. In Figure 10.2a, TT' represents the production possibility locus. The free-trade equilibrium occurs at the production point P_F and consumption point C_F. The imposition of the tariff takes the production point to P_T and consumption point to C_T. The welfare associated with the tariff equilibrium is indicated by U_T. Now suppose smuggling occurs. Smugglers offer the price ratio indicated by the slope of the line P_sP_s'. At this price ratio production occurs at point P_s and consumption at C_s. The welfare level in this case is indicated by U_s, but $U_s > U_t$; therefore smuggling raises welfare. In Figure 10.2b we illustrate the case in which smuggling lowers welfare. The diagram is self-explanatory.

Figure 10.3 represents the borderline case which shows the price ratio that provides the cut-off point, i.e. the point at which the welfare associated with the tariff equilibrium is the same as the welfare associated with the smuggling equilibrium. The production possibility locus is again TT': free-trade production equilibrium occurs at point P_F: and welfare level is indicated by U_F. Now suppose that a non-prohibitive tariff is imposed. This takes production to point P_T and consumption to point C_T. The welfare level is indicated by U_T. Our task is to find a smugglers' price ratio that gives the same welfare level as U_T. This price ratio is given by the slope of $P_s^*P_s^{**}$. At this price ratio production occurs at P_s^* and consumption at C_s^*. The welfare level associated with smuggling is the same as with the tariff equilibrium, i.e. $U_T = U_s^*$. For any price ratio flatter than $P_s^*P_s^{**}$ smuggling will be a welfare-increasing activity and for any price ratio steeper than $P_s^*P_s^{**}$ smuggling will be a welfare-reducing activity.

We can formulate the following theorems:

Theorem 10.1: The welfare level associated with smuggling cannot be

Figure 10.3

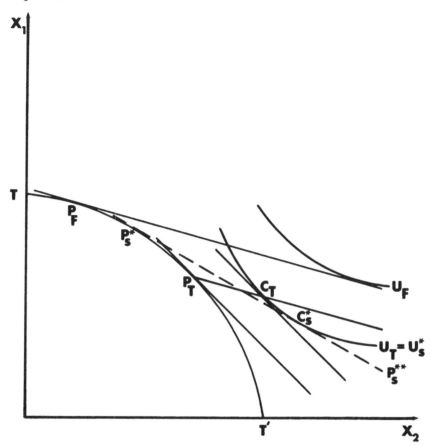

ranked uniquely *vis-à-vis* the welfare level associated with a non-prohibitive tariff, given the assumptions that smuggling occurs at constant costs, that the smuggling market is perfectly competitive and that there is no legal trade.

Theorem 10.2: The welfare level associated with smuggling is necessarily greater than that associated with a prohibitive tariff, given the assumptions that smuggling occurs at constant costs and is perfectly competitive.

An explanation of theorems 10.1 and 10.2 can be developed along the lines of the theory of customs union. Smuggling occurs either at the price ratio which is the same as the domestic tariff-inclusive price or a price which lies somewhere between the tariff-inclusive domestic price ratio and free-trade price ratio. In the latter case smuggling can be characterised as if the country has admitted a 'partner country' as an importer at a higher cost (where the lowest cost is provided by the free-trade solution). Since the importing cost is higher, smuggling imposes a terms of trade loss. However, there is a consumption and production gain because smuggling moves the economy towards the free-trade (optimal) position. The net result depends on whether the loss outweighs the gain and vice versa. Hence, it is not possible to rank uniquely the welfare level associated with smuggling *vis-à-vis* the tariff situation.

Now consider theorem 10.2, which states that the smuggling equilibrium is necessarily better than the prohibitive tariff equilibrium in welfare terms. The prohibitive tariff equilibrium is characterised by the absence of trade and the presence of only a single distortion. A well-known theorem of Bhagwati (15) states that 'a reduction in the degree of a single (only) distortion is successively welfare increasing'. The introduction of smuggling in the prohibitive tariff case results in the reduction of an only distortion, and hence is better welfare-wise than the prohibitive tariff situation. This case can also be discussed from the point of view of the theory of customs union.

10.3 Impact of Smuggling on Welfare When Legal Trade and Smuggling Coexist

So far we have confined our attention to cases in which smuggling results in the total elimination of legal trade. However, when $p_d = p_s = \bar{p}_\varrho(1 + t)$, then there is the possibility that smuggling and legal trade may coexist. In the previous section, we have already proved that when $p_d = p_s = \bar{p}_\varrho(1 + t)$ smuggling is worse welfare-wise than the tariff situation (assuming the absence of legal trade). It follows from this result that if smuggling coexists with legal trade then the welfare level associated with the smuggling situation must be worse than with the non-smuggling case. This happens because at $p_s = p_d = \bar{p}_\varrho(1 + t)$ smuggling results in trade at inferior terms of trade (production point in this case is the same under smuggling as in the case of tariff).

This result can be easily represented in terms of a diagram. This is done in Figure 10.4, where TT' is the production possibility locus. Free-trade production equilibrium occurs at P_F and consumption

Figure 10.4

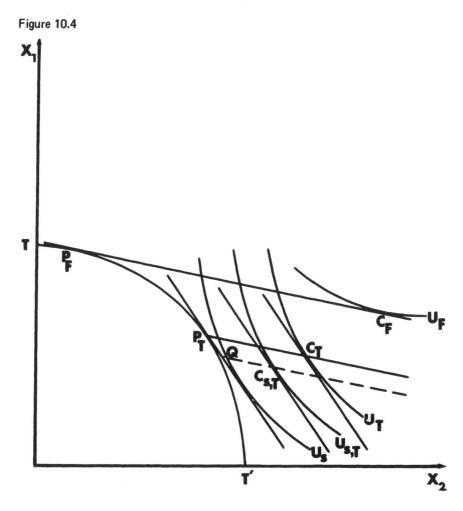

equilibrium at C_F. The imposition of a tariff takes production
equilibrium to P_T and consumption equilibrium to C_T. Now, if we
assume that the price ratio faced by smugglers is the same as the
tariff-inclusive domestic price ratio, then even in the smuggling case
production remains at point P_T. Smuggling takes the consumption
point to Q and legal trade and smuggling to C_{sT}. The welfare level
associated with the consumption point $C_{s,T}$ is indicated by $U_{s,T}$ which
is clearly below U_T. Thus, we can formulate the following theorem.

Theorem 10.3: If legal trade and smuggling coexist then the welfare level associated with this situation is necessarily worse than the non-smuggling situation, given the assumptions that there is a non-prohibitive tariff, constant costs in smuggling which equal the tariff-inclusive domestic price ratio and the existence of a perfectly competitive market for smugglers.

   In the results presented so far we have assumed that smuggling occurs at constant costs. Given this particular assumption, it is difficult to determine whether legal and illegal trade will coexist or not. If the assumption of constant costs is replaced by the assumption that smuggling occurs at increasing costs then it is quite easy to determine the existence of legal and illegal trade.

10.4 Impact of Smuggling on Welfare When Smuggling Eliminates Legal Trade and Smugglers Face Increasing Costs

In order to represent the case of smuggling at increasing costs, we have to draw a new smugglers' transformation curve. We shall retain the assumption that smuggling is a competitive activity. This is done in Figures 10.5a and 10.5b. The curves P_sS in 10.5a and $P_s'C'$ in 10.5b now represent the smugglers' transformation curves. These curves exhibit diminishing returns. In Figure 10.5a free-trade equilibrium occurs at production point P_F and consumption point C_F. The imposition of tariff takes production to point P_T, consumption to C_T and welfare to U_T. The line P_sC_s shows the domestic price ratio at which production and consumption take place under smuggling. The consumption point is intersected by the smugglers' transformation curve P_sS. Welfare level is indicated by U_s. Now in Figure 10.5a, $U_s > U_T$, hence smuggling is, welfare-wise, better than non-smuggling. The inferiority of the smuggling situation welfare-wise to the non-smuggling situation is demonstrated in Figure 10.5b. We now obtain the following theorem.

Theorem 10.4: The welfare level associated with smuggling cannot be ranked uniquely *vis-à-vis* the welfare associated with a non-prohibitive tariff, given the assumptions that smuggling occurs at increasing costs, that smuggling is a competitive activity and that there is no legal trade.

10.5 Impact of Smuggling When Smuggling and Legal Trade Coexist and Smugglers Face Increasing Costs

We now present the case in which legal and illegal trade coexist and smugglers face increasing costs. The activity of smugglers is again

Figure 10.5a

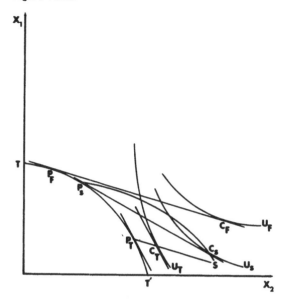

Figure 10.5b

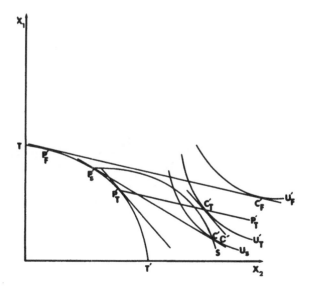

assumed to be competitive. In order that legal and illegal trade may coexist, we again need the condition that the price ratio that smugglers offer must equal the tariff-inclusive domestic price ratio. In Figure 10.6 this price ratio is represented by the slope of the line $P_T P'_T$. This line represents the average terms of trade for the smuggler. For smuggling equilibrium to occur the average terms of trade must equal the marginal terms of trade. This happens at point Q. Legal trade takes the consumption equilibrium to C_s. The welfare level associated with illegal and legal trade is indicated by U_s. Now $U_s < U_t$ and hence the coexistence of legal and illegal trade (smuggling) is worse in welfare terms than legal trade. The following theorem immediately follows.

Figure 10.6

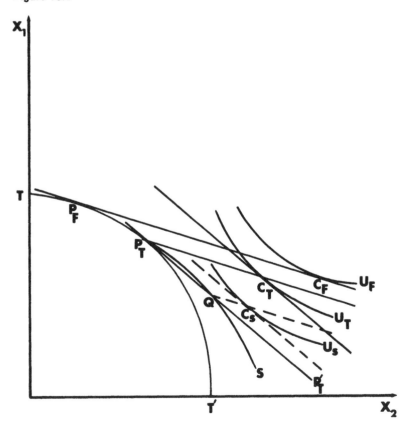

Theorem 10.5: The coexistence of legal and illegal trade is necessarily worse in welfare terms than legal trade, given the assumptions that there is a non-prohibitive tariff, increasing costs and perfect competition in smuggling.

The main conclusions that emerge from theorems 10.1 to 10.5 are the following. In the standard two-factor, two-commodity model of trade, if a non-prohibitive tariff eliminates legal trade then it is not possible to rank smuggling *vis-à-vis* non-smuggling in a welfare-wise comparison. If legal and illegal trade coexist as a result of a non-prohibitive tariff then the smuggling situation necessarily is welfare-wise worse than the non-smuggling situation.[8] Finally, if the tariff is prohibitive then smuggling is better necessarily than the non-smuggling situation.[9]

In the context of the inability to rank, welfare-wise, smuggling *vis-à-vis* non-smuggling, Bhagwati and Hansen express the view that 'smuggling becomes a welfare-reducing phenomenon contrary to common belief'. From the theoretical point of view the Bhagwati—Hansen result is interesting, but not surprising because, as remarked earlier, the comparison is between two suboptimal positions. Since from the theory of the second best we know that a unique welfare ranking is not possible, smuggling can be either welfare-increasing or welfare-reducing. More importantly, a lot of smuggling in less-developed countries occurs in commodities which have prohibitive tariffs. Of course, it is very difficult to judge empirically when a tariff is prohibitive. At least in the mind of the present author, the common belief is correct with regard to the prohibitive tariff, in which case smuggling does increase welfare.

10.6 Economic Expansion and Welfare in the Presence of a Tariff But No Smuggling[10]

In this subsection, we present a case in which economic expansion lowers welfare in the presence of a tariff, given the assumption that the country is small.[11] Though this result can be proved easily via the use of calculus, we shall only employ geometry for presenting the case. This approach has been adopted because the algebra does not provide any additional insight about the occurrence of 'immiserising growth'.

In Figure 10.7, TT is the pre-growth production possibility locus. Let us assume that the country is small, and thus it takes the international prices to be given: these are indicated by the slope of the line $P_T P$. The small country is assumed to have levied a tariff, which results

Figure 10.7

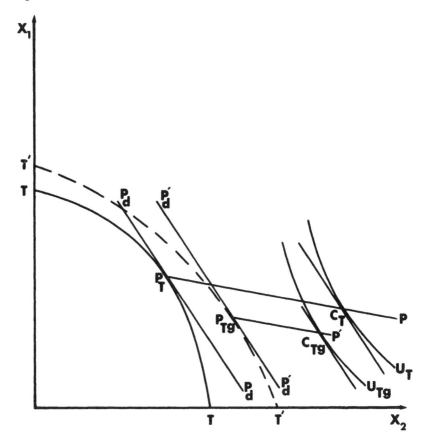

in production at P_T and consumption at C_T. At the position of
equilibrium DRS = DRT ≠ FRT. Let us now suppose that biased
economic expansion occurs, where the bias is assumed to be in favour
of the production of the imported commodity X_2. This expansion
results in the outward shift of the transformation curve. The post-
growth transformation locus is shown by $T'T'$. On this transformation
curve production occurs at P_{Tg} and consumption at C_{Tg}. Welfare is
indicated by U_{Tg} which is less than U_T, and hence growth is
immiserising. Note that due to the assumption of a small country, all
prices have been held constant.

The explanation of the above result runs along the following lines.
The imposition of the tariff in the pre-growth situation results in

production and consumption at suboptimal positions. The output of X_2, the protected sector, is higher than the optimal level due to the tariff. When import-biased growth occurs (at constant prices) at the point of equilibrium, the output of X_2 rises and that of X_1 falls. This further accentuates the production loss, which causes 'immiserising growth'. An alternative way of looking at this phenomenon is through the evaluation of national income at domestic and international prices. From Figure 10.7 it is obvious that national income falls in terms of international prices but rises in terms of domestic prices. Hence, at world prices the economy suffers a loss resulting in 'immiserising growth'.

10.7 Summary

In this chapter, we have examined some consequences of the imposition of a tariff in the small-country case. We have arrived at the following interesting results.

(1) The imposition of a tariff may result in smuggling.

(2) In the case of a non-prohibitive tariff the level of welfare associated with smuggling cannot be uniquely ranked with the welfare level associated with the tariff situation with no smuggling.

(3) In the case of a prohibitive tariff smuggling is better necessarily in welfare terms than the non-smuggling tariff situation.

(4) Economic expansion in the presence of a tariff (with no smuggling) may result in 'immiserising growth'.

All these results are significant for less-developed countries where tariffs are frequently used for various reasons.

Notes

1. It was the intention of the author to have two chapters in this part of the book, one dealing with smuggling and welfare and the other with illegal migration and welfare. The latter phenomenon also represents a kind of smuggling. However, so far the author has not been able to obtain any satisfactory results on illegal migration and welfare, hence the omission. The analysis of smuggling also ignores illegal trade in economic bads and assets.
2. A discussion of various arguments for protection is available in Black (11).
3. It has been demonstrated in the literature that a production goal is better attained with the help of a production subsidy rather than a tariff. The former

policy involves no consumption loss. The latter policy imposes both a production loss and a consumption loss; see Bhagwati and Srinivasan (10) and Corden (12).

4. This has been done in a pioneering paper by Bhagwati and Hansen (2). It is important to analyse smuggling also because it vitiates the accuracy of foreign trade statistics which are used for policy purposes. It is important to mention that smuggling is analysed purely as an economic phenomenon. Smuggling also raises moral and legal issues which are ignored in our analysis.

5. This simple device was introduced by Bhagwati and Hansen (2).

6. Bhagwati and Hansen (2) also analyse the case in which it is a non-competitive activity. In this case some assumption needs to be made regarding the residence of the smuggler. Bhagwati and Hansen assume the smuggler to be a non-resident. In the competitive case this problem does not arise because profits are zero.

7. Sheikh (8) has introduced the smuggling costs that involve the use of primary factors of production. To introduce smuggling costs in this manner a three-commodity model needs to be set up, which is beyond the scope of the present book.

8. This result does not carry over to the model which has been used by Sheikh (8).

9. Some other results in trade theory have also been examined in the presence of smuggling. References for these are provided at the end of the chapter.

10. It is not difficult to examine the impact of economic expansion on welfare in the presence of both the tariff and smuggling. Though this has been done in an unpublished paper by Beer and Hazari (1), such an analysis does not provide any new insights regarding the relationship between economic expansion and welfare. Hence the decision to restrict the discussion to the non-smuggling case.

11. This result was originally demonstrated by Johnson (14). The argument was extended to the case of monopoly power by Bhagwati (13).

References

On Smuggling

(1) Beer, J., and Hazari, B. R. 1975. Technical Progress, Smuggling and Welfare. Mimeographed. *La Trobe Economics Discussion Paper No. 13/75.*

(2) Bhagwati, J. N., and Hansen, B. 1972. A Theoretical Analysis of Smuggling. *Quarterly Journal of Economics*, Vol. 87 (May), 73–87.

(3) Bhagwati, J. N., and Srinivasan, T. N. 1974. Smuggling and Trade Policy. In J. N. Bhagwati (ed.), *Illegal Transactions in International Trade*. Amsterdam: North Holland.

(4) Bhagwati, J. N., and Srinivasan, T. N. 1974. An Alternative Proof of the Bhagwati–Hansen Results on Smuggling and Welfare. In J. N. Bhagwati (ed.), *Illegal Transactions in International Trade*. Amsterdam: North Holland.

(5) Bhagwati, J. N. (ed.) 1974. *Illegal Transactions in International Trade.* Amsterdam: North Holland.

(6) Johnson, H. G. 1972. Notes on the Economic Theory of Smuggling. *Malayan Economic Review*, Vol. 17 (April), 1–7.

(7) Ray, A. 1976. *Trade Protection and Economic Policy*, Chs. 5, 6. Delhi: Macmillan.

(8) Sheikh, M. 1974. Smuggling, Production and Welfare. *Journal of International Economics*, Vol. 4 (November), 355–64.

(9) Samuelson, P. A. 1954. The Transfer Problem and Transport Costs II: Analysis of Effects of Trade Impediments. *Economic Journal*, Vol. 64 (June), 264–89.

On Arguments for Protection

(10) Bhagwati, J. N., and Srinivasan, T. N. 1969. Optimal Intervention to Achieve Non-Economic Objections. *Review of Economic Studies*, Vol. 36 (January), 27–38.

(11) Black, J. 1959. Arguments for Tariffs. *Oxford Economic Papers*, new series, Vol. 11 (June), 191–208.

(12) Corden, W. M. 1957. Tariffs, Subsidies and the Terms of Trade. *Economica*, new series, Vol. 24 (August), 235–42.

On Immiserising Growth

(13) Bhagwati, J. N. 1968. Distortion and Immiserizing Growth: A Generalization. *Review of Economic Studies*, Vol. 35 (October), 481–5.

(14) Johnson, H. G. 1967. The Possibility of Income Losses from Increased Efficiency or Factor Accumulation in the Presence of Tariffs. *Economic Journal*, Vol. 77 (March), 151–4.

On a Change in the Degree of Distortion and Welfare

(15) Bhagwati, J. N. 1971. The Generalized Theory of Distortions and Welfare. In J. N. Bhagwati *et al.* (eds.), *Trade, Balance of Payments and Growth*. Papers in International Economics in Honour of C. P. Kindleberger. Amsterdam: North Holland.

11 CONCLUSIONS AND SOME GENERAL PROPOSITIONS IN THE PURE THEORY OF INTERNATIONAL TRADE AND DISTORTIONS

In this book we have examined several propositions in the pure theory of international trade, under various forms of market imperfections. Both the normative and positive aspects of the real theory of trade have been analysed within the distortionary framework. The approach adopted has been to introduce one and/or two distortions at a time and examine some standard propositions of international trade in the presence of such an imperfection. For instance, the optimality of free-trade policy is analysed in the presence of (a) factor price differentials, (b) externalities, (c) monopoly and (d) minimum real wage constraint. Obviously, an alternative procedure is to set up a very general model and examine all these cases as subsets. This procedure is analytically very appealing, but from a pedagogical point of view it is better to proceed from the particular to the general. Presented below are some general results which follow from the particular cases that we have considered.

It is possible to formulate some general propositions regarding the welfare consequences of imperfectly competitive markets. These generalised propositions do not exist in the positive branch of the theory of trade and distortions (although they are derivable from a general model). The following distortions have been considered:

   (i) factor price differentials;
  (ii) minimum real wage rates;
 (iii) Meade-type production externality;
 (iv) monopoly; and
  (v) tariff distortion in the small-country case.

The general theorems are:

(1) *Laissez-faire* is not the optimal policy in the presence of (i), (ii) and (iii).
(2) In welfare terms free trade cannot be ranked uniquely *vis-à-vis* autarky in the presence of (i), (ii), (iii) and (iv).
(3) The optimal policy in the presence of any type of distortion is

its removal by a suitable policy (this assumes that the distortion is capable of removal in principle).

(4) Economic expansion does not necessarily raise welfare in the presence of (i), (ii), (iii) and (v).

(5) A deterioration (improvement) in the terms of trade does not necessarily decrease (increase) welfare in the presence of (i), (ii) and (iii).

These results are derived on the basis of the 2 x 2 model presented in this book. They may or may not extend to more general models. Moreover, some of these results may extend to other distortions as well. For example, (1) can be proved in the presence of monopoly power in trade (a distortion not considered in the context of the optimality of the policy of *laissez-faire*).

Consequences 1 to 5 and the positive results presented in this book clearly show the importance and necessity of following optimal policies and the removal of distortions.

APPENDIX: THE DERIVATION OF THE OFFER CURVE AND STABILITY CONDITIONS

In Chapter 1 in a footnote, we mentioned that throughout the present book the Marshall–Lerner stability conditions will be assumed to be satisfied. To derive the Marshall–Lerner stability conditions, we not only need the offer curves of the two countries involved in trade but also the elasticity of the two offer curves at the point of equilibrium. In this appendix, we do four things: (a) derive the offer curve; (b) define the elasticity of the offer curve; (c) determine the equilibrium in terms of the offer curve diagram; and, finally, (d) derive the Marshall–Lerner stability conditions.

The Offer Curve

The offer curve (in the two-dimensional space) is defined as the locus of points that for each international price ratio between the commodities shows the quantity of exports the country would supply and the quantity of imports it would demand in exchange. The offer curve is also called the reciprocal demand and supply curve because it simultaneously shows the export supply that reciprocates with the import demand.

The offer curve can be derived from the excess demand conditions. Equations (1.3) and (1.4) of Chapter 1 show that domestic consumption equals output minus exports in the case of commodity 1 and output plus imports in the case of commodity 2. By rewriting equations (1.3) and (1.4), we know that $E_1 = X_1 - D_1$ and $M_2 = D_2 - X_2$. The offer curve, as stated earlier, is a locus of these excess demand points. Hence, if we plot these excess demand points, we can obtain the offer curve of the country. In Figure A.1b, on the horizontal axis we plot $E_1 = X_1 - D_1$ and on the vertical axis $M_2 = D_2 - X_2$, i.e. the home country's exports and imports respectively. The locus of these points BH is the offer curve. The excess demands are, of course, obtained from the supply and demand conditions as represented by the production possibility curve and the indifference map. The derivation of point L on the offer curve is explicitly being shown via the use of Figure A.1a. Let S in Figure A.1a be the position of self-sufficiency equilibrium, and hence at this point there is no excess supply or demand. Let pp′ represent the foreign price ratio. At this price ratio production

Figure A.1a

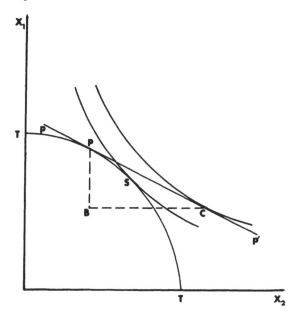

Figure A.1b

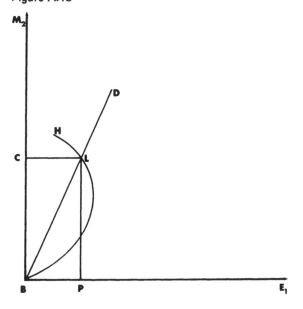

takes place at point P and consumption at point C. Obviously, BP of commodity 1 is exported in exchange for BC of commodity 2. The distance BP is plotted in Figure A.1b on the horizontal axis and the distance BC on the vertical axis. This gives us point L on the offer curve BH in Figure A.1b. The slope of the ray through the origin BD represents the price ratio between exportables and importables. In the diagram the slope of BD equals the slope of pp'. The self-sufficiency point in Figure A.1b is indicated by point B where there is no excess supply or demand. By following the procedure outlined for obtaining point L other points of the offer curve BH can also be derived.

Elasticity of the Offer Curve

In this section of the appendix we derive the elasticity of the offer curve OO' in Figure A.2. Elasticity of the offer curve is nothing other than the elasticity of demand for imports by the home country (ϵ_h) where by definition;

$$\epsilon_h = - \frac{d \log M_2}{d \log p} \quad \text{where} \quad p = \frac{p_2}{p_1} = \frac{E_1}{M_2}$$

This implies that:

$$\epsilon_h = - \frac{\dfrac{dM_2}{M_2}}{\dfrac{dE_1}{E_1} - \dfrac{dM_2}{M_2}} = \frac{1}{1 - \dfrac{M_2}{E_1} \dfrac{dE_1}{dM_2}}$$

Referring to point M_2^* in Figure A.2, dE_1/dM_2 is the inverse of the slope of the offer curve OO'. This is in diagrammatic terms $E_0 E_1^*/M_2^* E_1^*$. Now M_2/E_1 in terms of Figure A.2 at point M_2^* is $M_2^* E_1^*/OE_1^*$. By plugging these values in the formula for ϵ_h, we obtain the following elasticity for point M_2^*:

$$\epsilon_h = \frac{1}{1 - \dfrac{M_2}{E_1} \dfrac{dE_1}{dM_2}} = \frac{1}{1 - \dfrac{M_2^* E_1^*}{OE_1^*} \dfrac{E_0 E_1^*}{M_2^* E_1^*}} = \frac{1}{1 - \dfrac{E_0 E_1^*}{OE_1^*}}$$

$$= \frac{OE_1^*}{OE_0} > 1.$$

In geometrical terms the elasticity of the offer curve is given by OE_1^*/OE_0. At point M_2^*, $OE_1^* > OE_0$, and hence the offer curve at this point is elastic. By applying the above formula the elasticity of any

Figure A.2

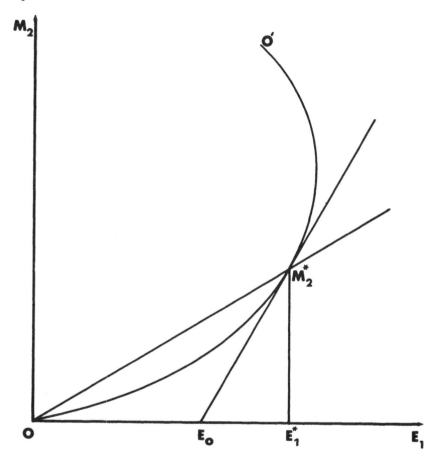

point on the offer curve can be obtained.

Determination of Equilibrium

In a similar fashion, the offer curve of the foreign country can also be constructed. Equilibrium is obtained at the point where the offer curves of the two countries intersect, for instance at point e in Figure A.3. The equilibrium terms of trade are indicated by Oe. The home country exports OE_1^* of commodity 1 in exchange for E_1^*e of commodity 2. If it is assumed that the home country is small, then of course the foreign offer curve is a straight line, indicating the fixed international price

Figure A.3

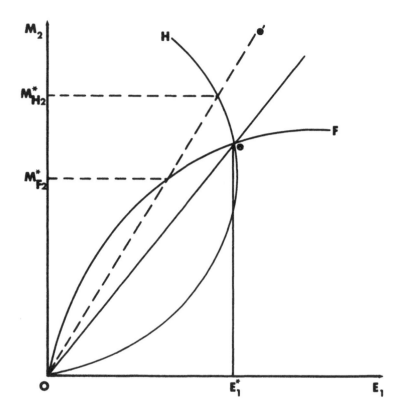

ratio that the small country faces.

Stability of Equilibrium

In this final section of the appendix, we consider the question of the stability of equilibrium of a point like e in Figure A.3. The stability condition is generally derived from the balance of payments equation (B) as follows:

$$B = E_1 - pM_2$$

Stability condition is obtained by differentiating the above equation with respect to p, the terms of trade. Stability of equilibrium requires that an improvement (decline in p) in the terms of trade results in a deficit in the balance of payments. This implies that $(dB/dp) > 0$ for stability. By differentiation, we obtain:

$$\frac{dB}{dp} = \frac{dE_1}{dp} - p\frac{dM_2}{dp} - M_2$$

Let us make the assumption that initially trade is balanced, so that $B = 0$. It follows:

$$\frac{dB}{dp} = M_2\left[\frac{p}{E_1}\frac{dE_1}{dp} - \frac{p}{M_2}\frac{dM_2}{dp} - 1\right]$$
$$= M_2\left[\epsilon_f + \epsilon_h - 1\right]$$

Now $M_2 > 0$, and hence for stability we require that $\epsilon_f + \epsilon_h > 1$, that is, the sum of the import elasticities should exceed unity. This is known as the Marshall–Lerner stability condition.

It is easy to show in terms of Figure A.3 the above stability condition. Let us suppose the terms of trade improve and the new terms of trade are given by Oe'. We are interested in the stability of point e. Now at the terms of trade Oe' the foreigners' supply of imports is indicated by $OM_{F_2}^*$. The home country's demand for imports is indicated by $OM_{H_2}^*$, and hence the improvement in the terms of trade results in a deficit of $M_{H_2}^* M_{F_2}^*$ in terms of commodity 2. This implies that $(dB/dp) > 0$ which is the stability condition, and thus e is a point of stable equilibrium.

References

On the Derivation of Offer Curve

(1) Meade, J. E. 1952. *A Geometry of International Trade*. London: George Allen and Unwin.
(2) Meade, J. E. 1965. *The Stationary Economy*. London: George Allen and Unwin.

On Stability Conditions

(3) Caves, R. E., and Jones, R. W. 1973. *World Trade and Payments: An Introduction*, Boston: Little, Brown. An excellent discussion of both stable and unstable equilibrium.
(4) Jones, R. W. 1961. Stability Conditions in International Trade: A General Equilibrium Analysis. *International Economic Review*, Vol. 2 (May), 199–209.
(5) Marshall, A. 1930. *The Pure Theory of Foreign Trade*. London: London School of Economics and Political Science.
(6) Mundell, R. A. 1960. The Pure Theory of International Trade. *American Economic Review*, Vol. 50 (March), 67–110.

AUTHOR INDEX

204

SUBJECT INDEX

For Product Safety Concerns and Information please contact our EU
representative GPSR@taylorandfrancis.com Taylor & Francis Verlag GmbH,
Kaufingerstraße 24, 80331 München, Germany

Printed and bound by CPI Group (UK) Ltd, Croydon, CR0 4YY
01/05/2025
01858351-0003